CONSTRUCTION CONTRACT DICTIONARY

LEONARD FLETCHER FRICS
REGINALD LEE MPhil FRICS
JOHN A TACKABERRY MA LLB *Barrister-at-law*

A COLLEGE OF ESTATE MANAGEMENT PUBLICATION

Distributed by
E & F N SPON LTD
LONDON   NEW YORK

First published 1981
by The College of Estate Management
Whiteknights, Reading RG6 2AW

distributed by E & F N Spon Ltd
11 New Fetter Lane, London EC4P 4EE

Published in the USA
by E & F N Spon
in association with Methuen, Inc.
733 Third Avenue, New York NY 10017

ISBN 0 902 13265 2 (cased)
ISBN 0 902 13263 6 (paperback)

PREFACE

This handbook is offered as an aid to those whose daily work (or study) brings them face to face with that peculiar set of English language words and phrases which forms a significant part of the vocabulary of the contractual aspects of construction. It is not advanced as a substitute for the standard texts on the law relating to construction contracts, but rather as a handy source of reference for dealing with the doubts which occasionally assail the student of or practitioner in construction about the meaning of some phrase or text.

The definitions must of course be read in the context of construction generally and of contract administration in particular. They are intended to be practical rather than scholarly, and whilst we believe every care has been taken in their compilation, the authors do not warrant their correctness. To the best of the authors' knowledge and belief the law is correctly stated as at 1 October 1980 and, except where otherwise described, references to the standard forms of building and civil engineering contract are to the latest editions available at that date. It is hoped to reissue the work from time to time, and suggestions for amendments and inclusions will be welcomed by the publishers.

Leonard Fletcher
Reginald Lee
John Tackaberry

London 1980

LIST OF CASES

The following are the abbreviations used in the report citations given below:

AC	Appeal cases
AllER	All England Law Reports
Bing	Bingham's New Cases
BLR	Building Law Reports
Ch	Chancery
EG	Estates Gazette
HBC	Hudson's Building Contracts
HL	House of Lords
KB	King's Bench
LGR	Local Government Reports
LT	Law Times Reports
Lloyd's Rep	Lloyd's Law Reports
QB	Queen's Bench
QBD	Queen's Bench Division
SALR	South African Law Reports
TLR	Times Law Reports
WLR	Weekly Law Reports

A & B Taxis Ltd v Secretary of State for Air (1922) 2 KB 336
AMF International Ltd v Magnet Bowling and G P Trentham Ltd (1968)
    1 WLR 1028
Acrow (Automation) Ltd v Rex Chainbelt Incorporated (1971) 1 WLR 1676
Alderslade v Hendon Laundry (1945) KB 189
Aluminium Industrie Vaasen BV v Romalpa Aluminium Ltd (1976) 1 WLR 676
Amalgamated Building Contractors Ltd v Waltham Holy Cross UDC (1952)
    2 All ER 452
American Airlines Incorporated v Hope (1974) 2 Lloyd's Rep 301
Andreae v Selfridge & Co Ltd (1938) Ch 1
Anns v Merton London Borough Council (1977) 2 WLR 1024
Appleby v Myers (1867) LR 2 CP 651
Archdale (James) & Co Ltd v Conservices Ltd (1954) 1 WLR 459
Arenson v Cassan, Beckman, Rutley & Co (1975) 3 WLR 815

Bacal Construction (Midland) Ltd v Northampton Development Corporation (1976)
    237 EG 955
Bank voor Handel en Scheepvaart NV v Slatford (1953) 2 All ER 956
Barker v Wimpey (1980) 1 Lloyd's Rep 598
Batty v Metropolitan Properties (1978) 2 WLR 500
Bennett & White (Calgary) Ltd v Municipal District of Sugar City No 5 (1951) AC 786
Bickerton & Son Ltd v N W Metropolitan Regional Hospital Board (1969) 1 All ER 977

STATUTES

Arbitration Acts 1950 & 1979
Architects' Registration Acts 1931 & 1938
Bankruptcy Act 1914
Bills of Sale Acts 1878 & 1882
Civil Liability (Contribution) Act 1978
Companies Acts 1948-1980

Copyright Act 1911
Corporate Bodies (Contracts) Act 1960
County Courts Act 1959
Defective Premises Act 1972
Health & Safety at Work Act 1974
Hire Purchase Act 1965
Insolvency Act 1976
Law of Property Act 1925
Law Reform (Frustrated Contracts) Act 1943
Law Reform (Married Women & Tortfeasors) Act 1935
Law Reform (Miscellaneous Provisions) Act 1934
Limitation Act 1939
Local Government Act 1972
London Building Acts (Amendment) Act 1939
Misrepresentation Act 1967
National Insurance (Industrial Injuries) Act 1965
Occupiers Liability Act 1957
Partnership Act 1890
Prevention of Corruption Acts 1889-1906
Public Health Act 1961
Sale of Goods Act 1979
Supply of Goods (Implied Terms) Act 1973
Town & Country Planning Act 1971 (as amended 1972)
Unfair Contract Terms Act 1977

ABANDONMENT

Refusal or failure to complete a contract; normally used in the sense of 'abandonment of works' by a contractor (ie ceasing work before substantial completion). Unless the abandonment amounts to an acceptance of a repudiation by the other party, or is expressly justified by the terms of the contract (eg most standard contracts have war provisions), it constitutes a breach of the contractor's fundamental obligation to complete and may be treated as a repudiation entitling the employer to rescind the contract and sue for damages.

Unexpected difficulties are no excuse for abandonment unless the change in circumstances is so radical that the contract is determined prematurely by the operation of the doctrine of frustration (a very rare occurrence).

The JCT Conditions of Contract contain express provisions entitling the employer to determine the contractor's employment 'if without reasonable cause he wholly suspends the carrying out of the Works before completion thereof'. This is additional to any common law rights and remedies which the employer may possess in respect of repudiation.

See Frustration, Rescission. Law Report: *Mertens v Home Freeholds Co* (1921).

ABROGATION

The act of annulling or repealing a law. It stands opposed to *rogation* and may be distinguished from *derogation*, which implies taking away only part of a law, and from *subrogation*, which denotes adding a clause to it.

In more general legal parlance, *derogation* is used to describe the clawing back of something granted; thus derogation from grant is a lessor or transferor trying to take back part of what he has granted by, for example, granting a third person a right of way over the land already granted. Similarly, *subrogation* is generally used to describe the doctrine under which an insurer, who has paid his insured, is then entitled to sue, in the insured's name, whoever caused the damage.

ABSTRACT OF PARTICULARS

This is the particular phrase used to describe the supplement to the GC/Works/1 Conditions of Contract which summarises any modifications to the printed conditions and gives the names or titles of the persons represented by the words 'Authority' and 'Superintending Officer' (SO), the date for completion, the amount of liquidated damages for delay and the length of the maintenance period. Both the JCT and ICE Conditions of Contract use an 'appendix' for a similar purpose.

ACCEPTANCE

Acceptance of a contractor's offer or tender creates a binding contract. The acceptance must be unconditional and if it suggests new terms it probably constitutes a counter-offer. Where the acceptance is made 'subject to formal contract', it is necessary to examine the offer or tender, and the 'acceptance', in order to work out from what is said in them whether or not the expression 'subject to' was intended to prevent a contract coming into force at all until the formal document was drawn up or executed (ie signed or sealed). This situation is described by the phrase 'condition precedent'. The alternative meaning of the expression 'subject to' is that it was intended that a contract should come into force immediately, and that, as one of the many obligations imposed by that contract, a formal agreement should be drawn up and/or executed in due course. This situation is described by the phrase 'condition subsequent'. Other examples of 'subject to' conditions are the familiar ones of 'subject to Ministry approval' and 'subject to loan sanction'.

Acceptance must take place within a reasonable time of the offer being made and in any case not later than the date stated for commencement of the contract. However, acceptance may be indicated by the conduct of the parties, such as starting work or allowing it to start. Also, where there have been lengthy negotiations and work has started prior to the execution of the formal contract, the terms may be construed as having retrospective effect. Where the offer is made in circumstances that contemplate acceptance by post, the acceptance is effective when posted and does not depend upon receipt.

See Law Reports: *Routledge v Grant* (1828); *Davies & Co Shopfitters Ltd v William Old* (1969).

ACCEPTED RISKS

This is a term used in the GC/Works/1 Conditions of Contract to describe the various natural and other hazards outside the control of the contractor which may affect the execution of the works.

The term currently embraces fire or explosion; storm, lightning, tempest, flood or earthquake; aircraft or other aerial devices or objects dropped therefrom; ionising radiations or contamination by radio activity; radioactive toxic, explosive or other hazardous properties of any nuclear assembly or component; riot, civil commotion, civil war, rebellion, revolution, insurrection, military or usurped power or King's enemy risks.

Provided the contractor has taken all reasonable precautionary measures, the Authority agrees to pay for loss or damage caused by any of the accepted risks and to grant an appropriate extension of time. The term should be distinguished from that of 'excepted risks' used in the ICE and JCT Conditions of Contract to describe comparable but not identical sets of hazards.

ACCESS

In order to carry out the functions assigned to him under the contract, the architect is given the benefit of the employer's implied right of reasonable access to the works. The JCT Conditions of Contract provide for the architect or his representative to have access not only to the works but also to the contractor's workshops. These Conditions of Contract also impose a duty on the contractor to secure a similar right of access, so far as possible, to sub-contractors' workshops and to do all things necessary to make such right effective.

See Interference.

ACCORD AND SATISFACTION

An agreement whereby a party who has performed the whole of his obligations under a contract agrees to waive the performance of some part of the obligations of the other party in return for a new consideration. The new consideration may take any form but it is usually a renouncement of a bona fide claim. Thus where a contractor has, or asserts that he has, completed the works and agrees to accept a sum less than the contract sum in consideration of the employer surrendering a claim for bad workmanship, the agreement is binding. In the absence of some such consideration, or quid pro quo, the agreement to vary the terms of the contract would have to be under seal in order to be binding.

See Law Report: *D & C Builders Ltd v Rees* (1966).

ACCOUNT

A financial statement of moneys due from one person to another. In construction contracts such statements take the form of Interim Valuations to determine the amounts payable to the contractor on account during the currency of the contract, and Final Accounts to determine the final balance due to the contractor.

Final Accounts set out the various adjustments required to be made to the contract sum in compliance with the terms of the contract. The expression 'Final Account' is not used in the JCT Conditions of Contract but is covered by several references against a marginal heading of 'Final Adjustment of Contract Sum'. The contractor is required to supply the architect with all documents necessary for this purpose, and any accidental inclusions or exclusions or arithmetical errors in the computations can be corrected even after the issue of the final certificate.

Daywork accounts are submitted by contractors in respect of varied work which cannot be properly measured and valued on the basis of the prices in bills of quantities. Such accounts give details of the prime costs of labour, materials and plant expended on the work with an addition for overheads and profit.

Company accounts are those accounts which companies are required by law to keep, showing all sums received and expended, all sales and purchases of goods, and the assets and liabilities of the company. These books of account must be at all times open for inspection by the directors of the company.

A further context in which the word may be used is where there has been a series of transactions between parties followed by an agreed balance payable by one party to the other, the agreed balance then being known as 'an account stated'.

ACTIVITY BILL OF QUANTITIES

See Bill of Quantities.

ACT OF GOD

The operation of natural forces which human foresight cannot be reasonably expected to anticipate. As the test is such a high one the occurrence of an act of God must be regarded as a very rare event.

The concept is pertinent to construction contracts in two respects; firstly, when the relevant occurrence will, by an express term of the contract, have the effect of relieving the contractor from his obligation to complete the works by the contract date for completion; and secondly, it is sometimes available to insurers as a defence to liability under insurance contracts.

See Force Majeure. Law Report: *Tennent v Earl of Glasgow* (1864).

ADJOINING OWNER

The owner of adjoining property (ie any site adjacent to or bordering on the site of construction works). The design of a building must have regard to the rights of adjoining owners, such as rights to light and to support.

Construction processes must be carried out in such a way as not to interfere unreasonably with any adjoining owner's enjoyment of his property. Failure to take proper steps to minimise noise, dust etc might be held to be a nuisance and provide grounds for an action for an injunction prohibiting the continuance of the nuisance and/or for damages. However, building operations are by their nature noisy and dirty and the steps which can be taken to reduce inconvenience to others will depend upon what is reasonable and practicable in the particular circumstances.

It should also be noted that the term is of some importance in the administration of the London Building Acts and the regulations made thereunder, and, in particular, in connection with party wall works and disputes.

ADOPTION

The exercise by trustees in bankruptcy, and liquidators, of the right to continue and complete contracts which are uncompleted at the time of the bankruptcy or liquidation.

Adoption will be presumed if the trustee in bankruptcy or the company in liquidation fails to respond, within twenty-eight days, to an application in writing from an interested party, for a decision to be made.

Although a trustee will be personally subject to all the terms of an adopted contract, a liquidator will not, as he acts in his official and not his personal capacity. Effectively this means that a party under contract with the company under liquidation may, if the contract is adopted, have preference over ordinary creditors in the winding up.

See Disclaimer. Legislation: Bankruptcy Act 1914; Companies Acts 1948-1980

ADVANCE

See Interim Payment.

ADVERSE WEATHER CONDITIONS

See Inclement Weather.

AFFIDAVIT

A form of evidence involving a written statement of fact (either known or believed) or of opinion, made during judicial or arbitral proceedings by a person who voluntarily signs and swears or affirms it.

AGENCY

An agent is one authorised expressly (ie in so many words) or impliedly to act as personal representative for another who is called the principal. As a result, the principal is bound by the acts of the agent in exactly the same way as he would have been had they been his own acts, provided that what the agent has done is covered by the authority he was given.

The relationship between principal and agent may be created by express appointment, or may be implied by law, or inferred from the conduct of the parties. It may also arise where one person, without previous authority, professes to contract on behalf of another who subsequently ratifies or adopts the contract made on his behalf. The extent of an agent's authority depends primarily upon the instructions he receives from his principal. He has implied authority to do as much as, and no more than, is reasonably necessary for and incidental to the execution of his express instructions. Provided he acts within his authorised capacity he incurs no personal contractual obligations to third parties. However, if he acts in excess of his authority without the knowledge of the person with whom he is dealing — and the latter suffers loss as a result — the agent may be personally liable for breach of warranty of authority.

The rights and liabilities as between principal and agent are laid down in a contract of agency, or, where not expressly stated, are ascertainable by reference to the general law of agency and to any applicable professional or trade custom. It is the duty of an agent to exercise for his principal's benefit such skill and capacity as he professes to have and not to let his own interests conflict with his obligations to his principal. The relationship of principal and agent is a fiduciary one (ie one in which mutual trust and trustworthiness is recognised by law as being at the heart of the arrangement) and it is the agent's duty to preserve utmost good faith (it is a contract *uberrimae fidei*) with his principal. If in the course of the agency the agent makes any profit or receives any benefit, he is deemed to have received such profit or benefit on behalf of the principal and must duly account for it. The Crown has even claimed (relying on this doctrine) the sums paid to a soldier as bribes for turning a blind eye to smuggling. The offer or acceptance of a bribe or secret commission by an agent is punishable as a misdemeanour under the Prevention of Corruption Act 1906.

An agent has no power to delegate his duties to a sub-agent except with the express or implied consent of the principal. Delegation may be implied where it is in accordance with professional custom, provided that it is not inconsistent with express instructions given by the principal to the agent.

The authority given by the principal to the agent may be ended by agreement between them or by performance — when the agent has fulfilled his duties; by revocation — subject to proper regard being given to the interests of the agent and third parties; or by operation of law — in the event of bankruptcy, insanity, death or imprisonment of the principal or agent.

An agent who commits a tort cannot rely on his role as agent to escape liability for a claim by the injured party. Thus the contractor who removes support from the adjoining owner's property will be liable to that owner — even if the removal of that support was inevitable if the works were to be carried out at all. In such a case the building owner will probably also be liable to the adjoining owner. Liability as between the contractor and the building owner would depend upon the terms of their contract. Thus, the relevant principles are: (1) that a person cannot excuse a tort by pleading that he was acting as agent for another; (2) that both principal and agent are jointly and severally liable in respect of a tort committed by an agent with the authority of the principal. The liability of a principal for his agent's torts depends upon the doctrine of authorisation. A person is usually not liable if he authorises another to do a lawful act and, in the course of doing it, such other person commits a tort, unless the relationship of master and servant also exists between them.

See Law Reports: *Summers v Solomon* (1857); *Doyle v Oldby Ltd* (1969).

AGENT

See Agency.

AGREEMENT

An expression by two or more persons of a common intention. The essence of an agreement is the *consensus ad idem* — consent to the same thing. A contract is an agreement, but not every agreement is a contract. In order that an agreement shall be legally enforceable as a contract, three conditions are essential: the agreement must relate to the future conduct of one or more of the parties; the parties must intend that their agreement is to be enforceable at law (eg an agreement to dine together is not usually intended to be actionable if one of the two backs out); and the agreement must be capable of performance without transgressing the law.

The use by some Football Pool promoters of the phrase 'this transaction is binding in honour only' is a good example of an agreement that is not intended to be legally enforceable and which is therefore not a contract.

ANTIQUITIES

Objects of historic interest. It is usual to declare in construction contracts that any such objects found on the site are the property of the employer. However, money, coin, gold, silver, plate and bullion found hidden in the ground would constitute treasure trove and belong to the Crown unless claimed by someone able to prove ownership.

APPROVAL

Construction contracts may provide that the work is to be carried out and completed to the approval of the employer or more commonly his agent, who is usually an architect or engineer. Such approval must not be withheld dishonestly or capriciously, and where the JCT or ICE Conditions of Contract are used, any withholding of approval for whatever cause may be reviewed by the arbitrator in the same way as any other decision of the agent. In the absence of express provision, approval is not regarded by the courts as a condition precedent to payment, the employer having a remedy in set-off or counter-claim in respect of defective work.

The JCT Conditions of Contract give a continuing right to the architect to order the removal from the site of work or materials which are not in accordance with the contract, and expressly restrict the value of work to be included in interim certificates to that which has been 'properly' executed. The amount certified may be challenged by the contractor, who has a right to immediate arbitration on the question of whether or not a certificate has been improperly withheld or is not in accordance with the contract. The employer is further protected from defective work by the right to require the contractor to make good defects after practical completion and during the defects liability period where the defects are due to materials or workmanship not in accordance with the contract.

Prior to the July 1976 revision of the JCT Conditions of Contract, the final certificate was, provided neither party had requested arbitration within 14 days of its issue, conclusive evidence that the works had been properly carried out and completed in accordance with the terms of the contract. The July 1976 revisions, also adopted in the 1980 edition, amended the scope of the final certificate which, in relation to approval, is now 'conclusive evidence that where the quality of materials or the standards of workmanship are to be to the reasonable satisfaction of the Architect/Supervising Officer the same are to such satisfaction ...'; this is a much less comprehensive provision than formerly.

Construction work is also inspected at various stages by the local authority building inspector to ensure compliance with the Building Regulations. Following the case of *Dutton v Bognor Regis UDC* (1972) as modified and explained in *Anns v Merton* (1977), it is clear that a local authority has to exercise care in formulating its policy as to inspection (ie the administrative level) and in carrying out any inspections which are made (ie the operative level). Failure to exercise a proper degree of care at either level may render the authority liable in negligence to a subsequent owner or occupier of the property if damage results. The position of the building owner is not clear but may be the same as that of the subsequent owner if the building owner is not also the builder. The case of *Anns v Merton* also made it clear that the contractor owed subsequent owners and occupiers a statutory duty to comply with the Building Regulations. It should also be noted that within Central London, Section 82 of the London Building Acts (Amendment) Act 1939 appears to impose on the District Surveyor the very onerous duty of 'ensuring' compliance with the relevant regulations.

ARBITRATION

A means of settling disputes otherwise than in a court of law by referring the matter in dispute to the independent judgement of one or more persons (ie arbitrators) specially nominated for the purpose; such judgement is called an award.

The parties to a contract may agree upon the person who is to act as arbitrator or merely upon the method of selecting an arbitrator (eg by subsequent agreement or by appointment by the President for the time being of the Royal Institute of British Architects). In some cases the arbitrator's agreement may provide for the appointment of two arbitrators who are required to appoint an umpire who will enter upon the reference should they fail to reach agreement. To avoid the risk of a complete re-hearing it is advisable for the umpire to sit with the two arbitrators throughout the reference.

A written agreement to refer present or future disputes to arbitration falls within the scope of the Arbitration Acts and, as such, cannot be revoked except by leave of a judge and then only in exceptional circumstances. If one party to the agreement commences legal proceedings, the other party may apply to the court to stay the action and enforce the arbitration agreement; the onus is then upon the party who commenced the proceedings to show good reason why the stay should not be granted. In general the court will refuse to stay the proceedings if the sole point at issue is one of law, or where more than two parties are involved — there being no procedural techniques in arbitration for joining third parties unless such are expressly provided in the relevant agreements to refer (eg the optional provisions in the JCT Conditions of Contract). If the arbitration agreement contains what is known as a *Scott v Avery* clause, namely one which provides that no right of action shall accrue in respect of any dispute until the dispute has been decided by an arbitrator, the court will stay the proceedings unless it can be shown that that provision has been waived.

In theory arbitration should be quicker and cheaper than the ordinary process of law, by virtue of the dispute being resolved by someone skilled in building matters and possessing personal knowledge of the processes and customs of the industry. Where an arbitrator's award is disputed on a point of law, the Arbitration Act 1979 now lays down procedures for obtaining a judicial review by the High Court. Any party to the arbitration, with the consent of the other parties or with leave of the Court (leave will only be given if the Court considers that the point of law could substantially affect the rights of the parties), may appeal to the High Court. The Court then has the power to order the arbitrator to give detailed reasons for his award except that where the award has been given without stating reasons the Court will not make such an order unless satisfied that before the award was made one of the parties gave notice to the arbitrator that a reasoned award would be necessary or that there was a special reason why such written notice was not given. Similarly, where a point of law arises during the reference, an application may be made to the High Court with the consent of the arbitrator or with the consent of all parties for the Court to determine the preliminary point of law before proceeding further. However, the Court will not entertain such an application unless satisfied that a decision on the point of law is likely to produce substantial savings in cost to the parties or that the question of law is one in respect of which leave to appeal would be likely to be given. The parties may agree in writing to exclude the rights of appeal provided in the 1979 Act but this is not to prohibit or restrict access to the Courts or their jurisdiction and would not apply to statutory arbitrations or where fraud is involved.

The court retains control over arbitration proceedings and may revoke the arbitrator's authority on the ground of interest, misconduct or bias. Section 24(1) of the Arbitration Act 1950 provides that it shall not be a ground for refusing an application to revoke the arbitrator's authority that the party making the application knew or ought to have known that the arbitrator by reason of his relation to the other party might not be capable of impartiality. Thus the practice of appointing the employer's architect to act as arbitrator is no longer sound.

It is usual for the arbitrator to call a preliminary meeting to decide procedure and to set a timetable — for example by arranging the date and place of the hearing — and the formal steps to be taken before the hearing. The occasion may also be used to attempt to clarify the issues in dispute. The arbitrator has many of the powers possessed by the court (eg the ordering of discovery of documents). Where expert witnesses are to be called they will usually be required to submit written reports setting out their views, as experts, on the particular points to which their expertise is relevant. The submission of such a report does not inhibit the extent of the evidence they may give when called, albeit that any substantial divergence between an expert's report and his oral evidence may throw considerable doubt upon his reliability.

Although the arbitrator has discretion as to the form of the hearing, it is usual in complex cases to adopt as nearly as possible the procedural rules of the High Court. At the hearing the claimant's representative addresses the arbitrator and calls his witnesses, each of whom is examined (ie questioned by the representative of the party on whose behalf he is giving evidence), cross-examined (ie cross-questioned by the representative of the opposing party), re-examined (ie questioned by the party calling him (if necessary) to clarify what has been said in cross-examination) and, if necessary, questioned by the arbitrator. The respondent then has a similar right to present his evidence. Then the respondent's representative sums up and is followed by the claimant's representative. The arbitrator usually closes the case by reserving his award, that is by stating that he will publish it in due course.

An arbitrator's award may be enforced by leave of the court as a judgement, or an action may be brought to enforce it. In certain circumstances the court has power to remit an award for the re-consideration of the arbitrator.

Certain Acts of Parliament provide for specified types of disputes to be settled by arbitral tribunals (eg the National Insurance (Industrial Injuries) Act 1965 provides for the setting up of a tribunal to determine claims for benefits under the Act).

See Case Stated. Special Case.

ARBITRATOR

See Arbitration.

ARCHITECT

'An architect is one who possesses, with due regard to aesthetic as well as practical considerations, adequate skill and knowledge to enable him (1) to originate (2) to design and plan (3) to arrange for and supervise the erection of such buildings or other works calling for skill in design and planning as he might in the course of his business reasonably be asked to carry out in respect of which he offers his services as a specialist' — the definition formulated by the Architects' Registration Tribunal and cited in *R v Architects' Registration Tribunal ex parte Jaggar* (1945).

The use of the title 'Architect' is restricted by the Architects' Registration Acts 1931 and 1938 to persons who are registered in the Register of Architects. However, there is no restriction on the performance of architectural functions and the JCT Conditions of Contract provide for the use of the alternative title 'Supervising Officer' where an unregistered person is appointed to undertake the duties of architect described in the conditions. The title 'Superintending Officer' is used similarly in GC/Works/1 — the general conditions of government contracts for building and civil engineering works.

The architect is engaged by the building owner to act initially as adviser and subsequently, on the letting of the contract, as his agent, his authority being strictly limited by the terms of his employment. A private architect has no implied authority to accept a tender on behalf of the employer, nor to vary the terms of the agreement between the employer and the contractor. Usually he is given express power to vary the works, but this power must be exercised in accordance with the provisions of the contract, and the employer is not bound if the 'extra' work is in fact part of the contractor's original contract obligation.

An architect, like any other professional man, owes the employer a duty to exercise a reasonable degree of skill and care in the carrying out of the work which he has undertaken. In the performance of certain of his contractual functions he must also act impartially as between the parties and not allow his judgement to be influenced by the employer. However, the long-established principle that an architect when certifying was acting in a quasi-arbitral capacity and was thus protected from liability in negligence was overthrown in *Sutcliffe v Thackrah* (1974) when the architect was held to be negligent for including the value of defective work in an interim certificate. The liability of architects is likely to be further extended as a result of statements made in other recent cases. In *Esso Petroleum v Mardon* (1976) Lord Denning MR stated *(obiter)* that a professional man's liability to his client existed in both contract and tort.

In *Sparham-Souter & Another v Town and Country Development (Essex) & Benfleet UDC* (1976) it was said that a cause of action in tort accrues not when the damage actually occurs but when the plaintiff first discovers it. If this be right, the limitation period for actions in respect of such matters as negligent design or supervision could run from the time when the plaintiff becomes aware of the defect, possibly many years after completion of the works. The *Sparham-Souter* action was another of the *'Dutton'* cases (after *Dutton v Bognor Regis UDC* (1972)), being a claim by a house-owner against a local authority for negligent inspection of a property in course of erection. It was reviewed by the House of Lords in *Anns v Merton* (1977) and the result was the creation of an

entirely novel test for determining the point from which time ran in *'Dutton'*
cases; namely the point at which danger to health and safety is imminent. As a
matter of practical common sense this is likely to be at or after the date on which
the defects appear. It is, however, difficult to apply this test to the position of
an architect, and all that can be said with confidence is that in the present
climate architects should assume that the law is at least as onerous as the decision
in *Sparham-Souter* suggested and make their arrangements accordingly.

The architect's contract with the employer is a personal one and thus
cannot be delegated without the employer's consent. In a case where an architect
delegated the design of a reinforced concrete frame to a nominated sub-
contractor, and the frame subsequently failed, it was held that there was no
implied right to delegate the duty of design. The RIBA Conditions of Engagement provide that the architect may recommend specialist sub-contractors for the
design and execution of any part of the work and that he shall be 'responsible for
the direction and integration of their design, and for general supervision, but that
nominated sub-contractors shall be solely responsible for the detailed design
entrusted to them'. However, in the absence of a collateral warranty or specific
agreement, the employer would be in difficulties if he tried to sue such a sub-
contractor for defective design.

So far as the architect's supervisory duties are concerned he is required to
give such supervision as is reasonable to ensure compliance with the contract and
enable him to give an honest certificate. He may by agreement with the employer
delegate the routine day-to-day supervision to a clerk of works, but is not
entitled to rely on the clerk of works' judgement for matters of substance.

Although as a general rule an agent is not personally liable to third parties
when acting for a principal, there are circumstances in which an architect may
incur liability to the contractor. These include breach of warranty of authority,
negligent misstatements and acts, and misrepresentation.

See Law Reports: *Leicester Board of Guardians v Trollope* (1911); *Hickman v
Roberts* (1913); *Concrete Construction Ltd v Keidan & Co* (1955); *Clayton v
Woodman & Sons* (1962); *Anns v Merton* (1977).

ARTICLES OF AGREEMENT

This expression is used in many circumstances in legal circles but in the construction industry it is the specific title given to the preliminary section of the
JCT Conditions of Contract in which the basic elements of the contract are set
out. The Articles name the parties to the contract and the persons who are to
carry out the respective functions of architect and quantity surveyor as described
in the Conditions, give the location and scope of the works by reference to
contract drawings and other documents, and express the agreement by the
contractor to carry out and complete the Works and by the employer to pay the
stipulated contract sum or such other sum as shall become payable in accordance

with the terms of the contract, and set out the provisions of the Agreement which shall be applied to the settlement of disputes by arbitration. Space is provided at the end of the Articles of Agreement for an appropriate attestation clause (ie for the signatures of the parties and their witnesses).

ARTISTS AND TRADESMEN

This term was used in the pre-1980 editions of the JCT Conditions of Contract to describe persons who had direct contracts with the employer, usually, but not exclusively, for the execution of work of a decorative or artistic nature (eg sculpture) which was not within the normal scope of building work and not usually included in construction contracts. As such work had sometimes to be carried out concurrently with that of the main contract, it was necessary to provide that the contractor should permit such persons to have access to the site and, where required, to include in the main contract for the provision of staging or other facilities for such artists and tradesmen.

The 1980 edition of the JCT Conditions of Contract abandoned the concept of artists and tradesmen and substituted provisions requiring the contractor to permit works to be carried out by the employer himself or by persons employed or otherwise engaged by him.

See Law Report: *Central Lancashire New Town Development Corporation v Henry Boot & Co Ltd* (1980).

ASSIGNMENT

The transfer of contractual rights or benefits to a third party, either by an act of the person initially entitled to those rights or by operation of law, is known as assignment.

A common example in building contracts is the assignment by the contractor of moneys due to him in consideration for financial accommodation. Contractual liabilities on the other hand can only be transferred with the consent of the other contracting party, and to be effective would have to involve arrangements which amounted to a three-way agreement. This situation is referred to as a 'novation'. Also vicarious performance of liabilities (eg sub-letting parts of the work), whilst generally permissible, differs from assignment in that the person actually performing the obligation cannot sue or be sued on the main contract, under which the rights and liabilities of the principals remain unaffected.

Assignment may be either statutory or equitable. A statutory assignment is one which meets the requirements of Section 136 of the Law of Property Act 1925 (ie it must be in writing and express notice in writing must have been given to the debtor). Assignments which do not meet these requirements may nonetheless be effective as valid equitable assignments. The main difference is that under a statutory assignment the assignee (ie the person to whom the debt is assigned) may sue on the contract in his own name, whereas in the case of an equitable assignment he must join the assignor (ie the party who did the assigning) in the action.

Although it is not essential to give notice to the debtor in an equitable assignment, it is desirable to do so in so far as it establishes priority over other assignees who have not given notice. In the event of bankruptcy or insolvency of the debtor, the assignee's claim is valid against the trustee or liquidator provided the moneys have actually been earned at the date of the bankruptcy or insolvency.

A provision (in the terms now used in the JCT Standard Form of Sub-contract) describing the contractor's interest in the retention money as 'fiduciary as trustee for the sub-contractor' has been held to create a valid equitable assignment in favour of the sub-contractor; a similar provision is contained in the JCT Conditions of Contract but in both cases the provisions give little or no protection since there is seldom (if ever) a separate identifiable retention fund to which the trust can attach.

Assignment can also arise by operation of law (eg upon bankruptcy or liquidation or upon the death of a contracting party).

See Law Reports: *British Waggon Co v Lea* (1880); *Nokes v Doncaster Collieries Ltd* (1940); *Davies v Collins* (1945).

ATTESTATION

The signing by a witness to testify that the document in question was signed by another in his presence. It is generally sufficient that the party acknowledges his signature to the witness when the witness signs.

AVOIDANCE

The act of withdrawing from a voidable contract. In certain circumstances the law gives a party to a contract the right to treat it as having no effect and avoidance is the act of so treating it.

See Misrepresentation, Rescission.

AWARD

See Arbitration.

BANKRUPTCY

An act of bankruptcy is committed by a debtor who fails to comply with a notice issued by a judgement creditor. Failing suitable arrangements with the creditor(s), the debtor is eventually adjudged a bankrupt and his property becomes vested in a trustee in bankruptcy for distribution amongst his creditors. An adjudication may subsequently be annulled by an order of discharge releasing the bankrupt from future liability in respect of those debts.

Bankruptcy relates to individuals and the procedures are governed by the Bankruptcy Act 1914 and the Insolvency Act 1976. A bankrupt individual has his property, including his current contracts, automatically vested in (ie it passes into the ownership of) his trustee in bankruptcy. Where a contract cannot be performed except by the bankrupt in person, the bankrupt may, if he is willing, complete the personal contract, but in such event the trustee may claim the proceeds of it. Bankruptcy does not by itself cause the termination of a contract, or cause a breach of it, since the trustee may obtain leave to continue the business of the bankrupt party in an attempt to minimise the final deficit.

Section 38 of the Bankruptcy Act provides for the vesting in the trustees of 'all goods being at the commencement of the bankruptcy in the possession, order or disposition of the bankrupt, in his trade or business, by the consent and permission of the true owner, under such circumstances that he is the reputed owner thereof'. Thus materials in the contractor's yard which have been paid for by the employer might well pass to the trustee in bankruptcy if they are not separately stacked and clearly marked as belonging to the employer. As stated in the case of *Fox re Oundle and Thrapston RDC v The Trustee* (1948) 'the conditions essential to the operation of this section are that the true owner of the goods should by leaving them in the possession, order or disposition of the bankrupt put him in a position by means of them to obtain false credit'.

Bankruptcies give rise to problems that are particularly intractable. The position has been complicated in recent years by the introduction, by suppliers of materials, of clauses to their terms of trading which seek to retain title to goods supplied until fully paid for, and by the decision of the House of Lords in *British Eagle International Airlines Ltd v Compagnie Nationale Air France* (1975), a case which had nothing to do with construction but which appears to be of general application in outlawing pre-insolvency arrangements designed to reduce or vary the rights given by the rules to the trustee or liquidator to assist him in his task of gathering in the assets.

See Insolvency, Liquidation. Law Reports: *Tout and Finch, re* (1954); *Aluminium Industrie Vaassen BV v Romalpa Aluminium Ltd* (1976).

BASIC PRICES

A term used in the fluctuation of price clause of the JCT Conditions of Contract to define the market prices of materials and goods upon which the rates in the contract bills are deemed to be based. The list of basic prices is appended to the bills of quantities and is normally restricted to the principal materials which will be used. The net amount of any difference between the basic price and the market price payable by the contractor is added to or deducted from the contract sum in the settlement of the final account.

BID

See Tender.

BILL OF APPROXIMATE QUANTITIES

See Bill of Quantities.

BILL OF QUANTITIES

A document setting out in schedule form the quantities and descriptions of the constituent parts of proposed works. It is prepared from drawings, specifications and other information relating to the design, and the work is usually measured and quantified in accordance with the rules of a specified method of measurement. In addition to the measured items, which are usually grouped in trades or work-sections, the bill includes preliminary items describing the contractor's general obligations and preamble clauses specifying the materials and workmanship for each trade or work-section. Prime cost sums are included for work to be carried out by nominated sub-contractors or for goods to be supplied by nominated suppliers, and provisional sums are included for work which cannot be entirely foreseen at the time of tendering.

The primary purpose of the bill of quantities is to provide a uniform basis for competitive lump sum tenders but, during the progress of the contract, it also serves as a schedule of rates for pricing variations. When used in conjunction with the JCT Conditions of Contract which incorporate quantities, the bill of quantities should be prepared in accordance with the principles of the Standard Method of Measurement of Building Works and is deemed to be an accurate representation of the quality and quantity of the contract works, any errors in description or quantity being subsequently corrected as variations. It should be noted that contrary to the normal legal presumption, Clause 2.2.1 of the JCT Conditions of Contract (similarly Clause 12 of the pre-1980 edition) gives precedence to the printed conditions by providing that 'nothing contained in the Contract Bills shall override or modify the application or interpretation of that which is contained in the Articles of Agreement, the Conditions or the Appendix', a provision the effect of which was confirmed by the decision in the case of *Gleeson v Hillingdon Borough* (1970).

Where the design has not been fully completed at the time of preparing the bills of quantities, tenders may be invited on the basis of a Bill of Approximate Quantities and the appropriate JCT Conditions of Contract adopted. The approach is similar to that envisaged by the ICE Conditions of Contract which specifically state that the quantities set out in the bill are not to be taken as the actual quantities and that remeasurement will be necessary to determine the correct quantities. In the case of civil engineering contracts both the bill of quantities and the specification are contract documents and must be read together to determine the quality and quantity of the work, whereas under the JCT (with Quantities) Conditions of Contract the bill of quantities serves both functions.

Variations on the traditional grouping of items into trades or work sections have been developed to cater for specific purposes. These new forms include Elemental, Operational, Activity and Locational groupings.

Elemental bills of quantities were developed to aid cost planning and are divided into functional elements (ie parts of the building, such as the roof, which always perform the same functions irrespective of the method of construction or materials used).

Operational bills of quantities were devised in an attempt to relate the estimator's prices more directly to site processes. These bills are sub-divided into discrete operations representing the work done by one man or a gang of men on a specific task. Provision is made for the labour content of each operation to be priced as a lump sum, the materials being separately measured and priced. However, this method departs fundamentally from the principles laid down in the Standard Method of Measurement which are based essentially on the measurement of completed parts of the building rather than work processes. To overcome this difficulty the Activity bill of quantities was developed in which the breakdown into operations is retained but the work within each operation is measured and described in accordance with the Standard Method of Measurement.

Locational bills of quantities were also developed to assist in the more accurate pricing of items by scheduling the quantities of work in different locations (ie positions within the contract works) separately.

See Law Reports: *Bryant & Son Ltd v Birmingham Hospital Saturday Fund* (1938); *Gleeson v Sleaford UDC* (1953); *Farr v Ministry of Transport* (1960).

BILL OF SALE

A deed assigning chattels either by absolute assignment, when possession must be transferred, or by way of security for a debt when possession is retained by the debtor. The latter kind must be registered and must comply with the Bills of Sale Acts 1878 and 1882.

See Bills of Sale Acts 1878 and 1882.

BILL OF VARIATIONS

A priced statement of variations in contract works. What will constitute a variation will depend on the contract terms. For example, Clause 13.1 of the

JCT Conditions of Contract defines 'variations' as embracing the alteration or modification of the design, quality or quantity of the Works as shown upon the Contract Drawings and described by or referred to in the Contract Bills, as well as the addition, alteration or omission of any obligations or restrictions imposed by the Employer in the Contract Bills in regard to access to the site or use of any specific parts of the site, limitations of working space, limitations of working hours, and the execution or completion of the work in any specific order. These conditions also provide that if in the Contract Bills there is any departure from the prescribed method of preparation or any error in description or in quantity or omission of items, then such departure or error or omission shall not vitiate the Contract but the departure or error or omission shall be corrected and such correction shall be treated as if it were a variation.

Pricing of the variations again depends upon the contract terms. For example, under the JCT Conditions of Contract, where the contract documents include bills of quantities, the prices in the bills are used for valuing varied work of a similar character executed under similar conditions. If the nature or method of execution of the varied work differs from that described in the bills, the bill prices are used as a basis for building up new rates, or a fair valuation is made, or, if the work is not capable of being measured, it is charged on a time and materials (or daywork) basis. Under the 'without quantities' version of the JCT Conditions of Contract the contractor is required to supply a schedule of rates for the purpose of valuing variations.

The JCT Conditions of Contract place a duty on the quantity surveyor to prepare the final Valuation of Variations not later than the end of the 'period of final measurement and valuation' stated in the Contract. This runs from the date of practical completion and the contract provides for it to be six months unless the parties express a different period.

BOND

A contract under seal binding a person (the obligor) to pay a sum of money to another (the obligee). The most common type is the 'conditional bond' which has a condition attached to the effect that if the obligor does or forbears from doing some act the obligation is void. Thus, in the case of performance bonds where the obligor guarantees due completion by the contractor, the obligor's promise to pay the employer the stated sum is conditioned to determine on certified completion.

As the obligor (or surety) may be released from his obligation by changes in the contract guaranteed, it should be provided that the guarantee will not be rendered void by variations in the contract work, extensions of time and other concessions granted to the contractor. Failing this it would be necessary to inform the surety of every change, no matter how minor, to the original contract requirements.

See Guarantee.

BONUS CLAUSE

Building and civil engineering contracts sometimes provide for the payment of a bonus to the contractor for early completion. This may be expressed as a stated sum per day, week or month that actual completion precedes the stipulated completion date, or as a fixed sum of money payable for completing before the specified date. The inclusion of such a clause needs careful consideration and the remainder of the contract should be minutely examined to see what provisions might impinge on the bonus clause. For example, under the JCT Conditions of Contract the effect of operating the extension of time clause would have to be considered. Delay by the employer which prevents the contractor from earning the bonus may entitle the contractor to recover the amount of the bonus as damages for breach of contract – *Bywaters v Curnick* (1906).

Incentives in relation to economic working are usually incorporated in target and cost-reimbursement contracts where the difference between the actual cost ascertained on a cost-plus basis and the estimated target cost is shared between the employer and the contractor in an agreed way. If the actual cost is less than the target the proportion of the saving payable would amount to a bonus, whilst if the actual cost is greater than the target the diminution in the amount payable would amount to a penalty (to use the term in a non-legal sense).

Difficulties are frequently encountered in the administration of contracts containing bonus clauses for it is rarely possible to advance the completion of the contract works without some commensurate effort being made by the employer's consultants, who will not be parties to the arrangement. Bonus clauses are thus best avoided unless the employer sees a significant benefit in earlier completion and his consultants confirm their willingness to collaborate. In almost all cases it is better simply to make the earlier completion date the contract completion date and to amend the contract sum by the amount of the bonus; the contract is then administered in the normal way.

See Liquidated Damages.

BREACH OF CONTRACT

A refusal or failure by a party to a contract to perform his obligations. The breach gives the other party a right of action for damages or, in some cases at the court's discretion, for specific performance. The breach may be a renunciation of a fundamental term or condition amounting to a repudiation and entitling the innocent party to treat the contract as at an end or it may be non-observance of a less important term which would merely entitle the injured party to damages. Specific performance is rarely granted in building cases in that damages usually provide adequate compensation, and also because the court is reluctant to undertake the supervision of work over a prolonged period.

Usually there are express provisions in construction contracts laying down the procedures to be followed and the damages recoverable for specified breaches (eg power to determine the contractor's employment for wholly suspending the execution of the works and recovery of liquidated damages for delayed completion). Where these provisions are expressed to be without prejudice to any other rights or remedies, the injured party may additionally pursue his rights at common law. Thus where a default constitutes a fundamental breach, the party adversely affected would be entitled to rescind the contract and to sue for ordinary damages.

See Rescission.

BUILDER

See Contractor.

BUILDING OWNER

See Employer.

BUILDING REGULATIONS

The Building Regulations 1976 provide a uniform national system of building control replacing the local byelaws which hitherto were produced by individual local authorities. The Building Regulations are issued by the relevant ministry under the provisions of the Public Health Act 1961 and apply to new buildings and to existing buildings where a material change of use is proposed. They control the use of materials, structural design, natural lighting and ventilation, open space around buildings, and drainage and sanitation. Compliance with them is obligatory and a failure by the contractor to observe them may lead to an action for breach of statutory duty by any party injured as a result of the default.

The Building Regulations are in the process of being superseded by regulations made in pursuance of Part III of the Health and Safety at Work Act 1974. This Act gives wider powers to make regulations with respect to the design and construction of buildings including measures necessary to secure the health, safety, welfare and convenience of persons using buildings or who may be affected by them, to further the conservation of fuel and power and to prevent the waste, undue consumption, misuse or contamination of water. The new regulations will also apply to Inner London which at present has its own constructional byelaws.

See Byelaws. Law Report: *Anns v Merton* (1977).

BYELAWS

A law made by a subordinate body (eg a local authority or public utility corporation) under powers granted by Parliament for the control of specified activities.

Byelaws made by local authorities must be approved by the relevant Government Minister, although such byelaws are nowadays usually in a standard, or largely standard, form put out by the Ministry. In any case it would be most unlikely that a local authority would make a byelaw that had not been scrutinised and passed by the Ministry in advance; thus approval is virtually automatic.

See Building Regulations. Law Reports: *Townsend v Cinema News* (1959); *One Hundred Simcoe Street v Frank Burger Contractors* (1968).

CAPACITY TO CONTRACT

The ability to enter into a binding contract. Every party to a contract must be legally capable of incurring the contractual obligation which the agreement purports to impose.

There are certain persons who by reason of personal disability have a diminished ability to contract or can only contract subject to certain rules. Cases of contractual incapacity include infants, corporations, lunatics or persons of unsound mind. Thus, in general, a contract is only binding on an infant (ie a person under 18 years of age) if it relates to necessaries; a corporation can only make (through its agent) such contracts as are within its power to make; and a person of unsound mind can avoid liability if he can show that the other party was aware of and took advantage of his mental condition. However, an undischarged bankrupt may contract without informing the other person that he is an undischarged bankrupt, provided he does not obtain credit beyond the prevailing statutory limit (currently £10), or trade under a name other than that under which he was adjudicated bankrupt.

See Contract.

CASE STATED

The process by which, prior to the Arbitration Act 1979, an arbitrator formulated a question of law arising in an arbitration (and upon which one of the parties had asked for a case to be stated) along with the relevant findings of fact, and, where appropriate, alternative awards. Any party could then apply to the High Court for its decision on the point of law. This was in accordance with the provisions (since repealed) of the 1950 Act that 'an arbitrator or umpire may, and shall if so directed by the High Court, state (1) any question of law arising in the course of the reference or (2) an award or any part of an award in the form of a special case for the decision of the High Court'.

The case stated procedure is still prescribed by the GC/Wks/1 Conditions of Contract in respect of contracts under Scottish Law — to which it was introduced by the Administration of Justice Act 1972.

CASH DISCOUNT

The amount by which a sum due to be paid is reduced in return for payment on or before a specified date. Such discounts are usually expressed as a percentage of the sum due and related to a period of days, weeks or months, either from when the goods are delivered or from when they are invoiced.

Cash discounts should be distinguished from trade discounts, which are reductions from the published or commonly quoted price of goods which are granted to specific purchasers by virtue of their commercial standing *vis-a-vis* the seller. Trade discounts are frequently expressed as a percentage of the gross value of an account, and whilst not usually conditional upon payment by a given date, may be related to an agreed volume of trade between the buyer and the seller.

CERTIFICATE

The means whereby the architect or engineer expresses a satisfaction, opinion or judgement required of him by the terms of the contract. Certificates are usually in writing, but in the case of *Elmes v Burgh Market Co* (1891) it was held that where there is no express provision for the architect to give a written certificate, an oral statement is sufficient. Whether written or not, a certificate must, to be effective, be given in accordance with any time restrictions provided by the contract.

Certificates usually relate to some act or omission by the contractor (eg the achievement of, or failure to achieve, practical completion of the works) or to a sum of money due to be paid. Those dealing with money fall into two categories:

1. Interim or progress certificates which are issued at monthly or other agreed intervals and which authorise payments on account by the employer to the contractor. They are usually based upon the value of work properly executed and materials on site and show amounts previously certified or paid and any sums retained under the terms of the contract. The values incorporated in such certificates are recognised to be approximations only and, in the absence of express provision to the contrary, are not binding as to amount. Similarly, an interim certificate is not evidence of the contractual adequacy of the work to which it refers, although in the case of *Sutcliffe v Thackrah* (1974), when a contractor's bankruptcy prevented the recovery of an overpayment, the architect was held liable in negligence for including the value of defective work in an interim certificate.

2. Final certificates which, as well as stating the sum to be paid in settlement of the contract, also express the satisfaction of the architect or engineer that the work has been completed in accordance with the contract. Such certificates may be expressly made binding and conclusive and thus preclude any appeal by the parties to the courts or to arbitration. In order for the certificate to be conclusive evidence in subsequent proceedings,

there must be express words in the contract making it so and it must be issued in the form and at the time required by the contract.

A certificate may be set aside if the certifier has any unusual unknown interests or if he fails to act independently. Thus in *Hickman v Roberts* (1913) a final certificate was set aside because the architect had allowed himself to be unduly influenced by the employer. In some cases a certificate is a condition precedent to the employer's right to take some action (eg under the JCT Conditions of Contract the right to deduct liquidated damages is dependent on the prior issue of a certificate stating that the work ought reasonably to have been completed by the date set for completion, or any extended date). Similarly, under the JCT Conditions of Contract, the right of the employer to pay a nominated sub-contractor direct is dependent upon certification by the architect that the contractor has failed to provide reasonable proof of discharge of an earlier interim payment directed by the architect to be made to the nominated sub-contractor.

A distinction should be made between the functions of a certifier and those of an arbitrator. A certifier exercises his own skill and judgement in deciding some matter upon which the terms of the contract require him to give an opinion and thus prevent a dispute from arising. On the other hand, an arbitrator is called upon to resolve a dispute which has already arisen between the parties and in so doing he calls witnesses and hears evidence. As laid down in *Arenson v Casson, Beckman, Rutley & Co* (1975), an essential prerequisite for a valuer (or certifier) to obtain immunity from liability in negligence is that by the time the matter is submitted to him there should be a formulated dispute between the parties which his decision is required to resolve. This followed the judgement in the case of *Sutcliffe v Thackrah* (1974) which rejected the notion that architects have a special immunity from liability for negligence when certifying.

See Law Reports: *Tharsis Sulphur & Copper Co v McElroy & Sons* (1878); *Royston UDC v Royston Builders Ltd* (1961); *Kaye (P & M) v Hosier & Dickinson* (1972).

CHATTELS

A French word meaning 'goods'. Chattels may be classified as either 'personal chattels' or 'chattels real'. Personal chattels include all types of movable property or effects (eg furniture, jewels, animals etc). Chattels real are estates or interests in or arising out of land, except freeholds. The difference between chattels real and freeholds consists for the most part in the fixity of their duration. Thus a leasehold interest which has a fixed duration is a chattel real whilst a freehold (which does not have a specified duration) is not so classified.

CIVIL COMMOTION

In a case which was concerned with fire insurance, the term was interpreted as meaning 'an insurrection of the people for general purposes, though it may not amount to a rebellion' *(Langdale v Mason* (1780)). It has also been described as a stage between a riot and a civil war. The element of turbulence or tumult is an essential ingredient; an organised conspiracy to commit criminal acts where there is no tumult or disturbance until after the acts does not amount to civil commotion.

CLAIMS

This is the term applied to demands by the contractor for additional payments to which he believes he is entitled under the terms of his contract or for damages for breach of the contract. Although the JCT Conditions of Contract do not specifically use the term 'claim', the contractor is required by Clause 26 to make written application to the architect stating that he has incurred or is likely to incur direct loss and/or expense in the execution of the contract for which he would not be reimbursed by a payment under any other provision of the contract because the regular progress of the Works or any part thereof has been or is likely to be materially affected by any one or more of a number of prescribed matters.

It will be noted that recovery under Clause 26 is directly linked with the material affectation of regular progress of the Works; the only other provision for similar recovery is in Clause 34 which prescribes actions to be taken by the contractor upon the discovery of antiquities. As it would appear to be quite possible for a contractor to be put to expense as a consequence of acts or omissions of an employer, or his agents or others for whom he is responsible, which do not materially affect regular progress of the Works, the contractor's remedy in such cases would have to be by way of an action for damages for breach of the contract — providing his claim for appropriate reimbursement was refused by the employer or his agent.

The JCT Conditions of Contract place the responsibility for ascertaining the amount of the loss or expense on the architect or, if he so instructs, the quantity surveyor, the contractor being obliged to submit, on request, such details of his loss and/or expense as are reasonably necessary for the ascertainment to be made. Similar provisions are contained in the ICE Conditions of Contract but in addition the contractor is required to keep such contemporary records as are necessary to support his claim and to make this information available to the engineer; also the onus is placed on the contractor to submit interim accounts giving detailed particulars of the amount claimed and further accounts giving the accumulated total of the claim.

CLERK OF WORKS

A person appointed by the employer, usually on the recommendation of the architect, to undertake the day-to-day inspection of building work under the direction of the architect. His duties are usually restricted to ensuring that the work done by the contractor is technically satisfactory in accordance with the contract requirements and to reporting any deviations from the technical requirements of the contract to the architect.

The qualifications of clerks of works vary, but normally they are tradesmen who have risen to the rank of foreman and had many years' practical experience of building. Resident engineers on civil engineering contracts perform the functions of clerks of works but generally have wider responsibilities and may be fully qualified engineers.

See Inspector.

COLLATERAL WARRANTY

See Warranty.

COLLUSION

An agreement between two or more persons to act in an improper manner in order to deceive a third party or the court. A certificate may be set aside if it can be shown that there has been collusion between the certifier and one of the parties to a contract with intent to defraud the other party.

COMMISSION

This is a payment made to an agent in respect of services rendered. However, it is illegal for one party to a contract to offer or to give any secret commission or other consideration to the agent of the other party in order to induce him to do or to forbear from doing any act in relation to the business of his principal (Prevention of Corruption Act 1906). Thus receipt by the architect, engineer or surveyor of any secret commission from the contractor would warrant instant dismissal of the offending party, recovery of the commission by the employer and release of the employer from any liability to pay for the agent's services.

The JCT Conditions of Contract for local authority use expressly empower the authority to determine the contractor's employment in such cases, whether the offering or giving of the secret commission was made with or without the contractor's knowledge by any persons in his employ or acting on his behalf. There is also a similar provision in the GC/Works/1 Conditions of Contract.

COMPANY

A company is a legal entity with an existence quite distinct from the persons who may from time to time form its membership. It may be incorporated by charter, special Act of Parliament or registration under the Companies Acts. Those registered under the Companies Acts are known as 'registered companies' and are usually 'limited' (ie the liability of the members for the debts of the company is limited by shares or guarantee). Such companies may be either 'public' or 'private', the main distinction being that a private company is prohibited from inviting the general public to buy its shares.

The promoters of a company must obtain the minimum number of sub-scribers — two for a private company and seven for a public company — and file the following documents with the Registrar of Companies; (1) a Memorandum of Association stating the objects of the company; (2) Articles of Association setting out the regulations governing the relations between the members; (3) a Statutory Declaration that the requirements of the Companies Act 1948 have been complied with and a statement of the nominal capital. When satisfied that everything is in order the Registrar issues a Certificate of Incorporation.

Where it is intended to obtain capital from the public, a prospectus must be issued in compliance with the requirements of the Companies Act. The most common shares are preference shares, which entitle the holder to a fixed rate of dividend, and ordinary shares, for which the dividend is determined after deducting payments to preference shareholders from trading profits. Every company must hold an annual general meeting and present a professionally audited balance sheet and profit and loss account.

The contractual capacity of a company is restricted to the objects stated in its Memorandum of Association and any contract outside the scope of the objects for which the company was formed is void. However, if the other contracting party was unaware of the irregularity he may be protected by the rule stated in *Royal British Bank v Turquand* (1856) (ie that provided the Memorandum and Articles contain nothing inconsistent with the proposed contract the other party is entitled to assume that internal formalities have been complied with and the contract is binding on the company).

It should be noted that as a company is an artificial person it can only act through its appointed agents whose authority is defined by the Articles of Association. If an agent exceeds his authority and thereby induces another to enter into a contract which is void for want of authority, he may himself become liable for breach of warranty of authority.

See Vicarious Liability. Legislation: Companies Acts 1948-1980.

COMPLETION

This term connotes a state of readiness of the building for immediate occupation even though some minor work may be outstanding.

This condition is described as 'practical completion' in the JCT Conditions of Contract and 'substantial completion' in the ICE Conditions of Contract. The date of its achievement is identified by a certificate of the architect or engineer and marks the commencement of the defects liability or maintenance period.

Extensive building contracts may contain provisions for 'phased completion' but in such cases the definition of the phases and the related rights and obligations of the parties in relation to them must be clearly stated. In the case of *Gleeson v Hillingdon Borough* (1970), where the bills of quantities provided for completion in stages but the Appendix to the JCT Conditions of Contract provided only for completion at one time, it was held that liquidated damages could not be deducted until the expiry of the period shown in the Appendix. This was based on the strict wording of Clause 12 of the Contract Conditions that 'nothing contained in the Contract Bills shall override, modify or affect in any way whatsoever the application or interpretation of that which is contained in these conditions'. Supplementary conditions in the form of a 'Sectional Completion Supplement' are available for use with JCT Conditions of Contract when required.

See Law Reports: *Williams v Fitzmaurice* (1858); *Appleby v Myers* (1867); *Hoenig v Isaacs* (1952); *English Industrial Estates v Wimpey* (1973).

CONDITION

When the term is used formally it refers to a vital undertaking in a contract, breach of which constitutes a repudiation entitling the other party to rescind the contract (eg abandonment of the work by the contractor before substantial completion without lawful excuse). Similarly, less important provisions of the contract are strictly called 'warranties', breach of which merely entitles the innocent party to damages.

The term may also be used in the sense of a condition precedent, making the rights or duties of the parties dependent upon the happening of some event (eg the payment of money being conditional upon the issue of a certificate), or a condition subsequent, whereby it is agreed that their rights or duties will be terminated by the occurrence of some event (eg the mutual abandonment of a contract upon the outbreak of war).

Both 'condition' and 'warranty' are used casually by both lawyers and laymen to mean 'terms', and reliance upon the name attributed to a particular provision would be unwise. Thus the forty 'conditions' of the JCT Conditions of Contract are not all (or even largely) conditions in the strict sense. Accordingly a court will look at the substance of an obligation to ascertain whether, in the strict sense, it is a condition or a warranty.

CONDITION PRECEDENT

See Condition.

CONDITIONS OF CONTRACT

The detailed provisions incorporated in the contract, laying down the rights and duties of the parties, the functions of the architect/engineer and other persons connected with the contract, and the procedures for administering the contract. It is usual to adopt one of the standard printed sets of conditions for work of any substance in that it not only avoids the expense of producing a special set of conditions but also introduces a greater degree of certainty into the contractual relationship between the employer and the contractor.

The more common standard forms are those issued by the Joint Contracts Tribunal (for building works and for associated sub-contracts), the Institution of Civil Engineers (for civil engineering works), and the Department of Environment (for government building and engineering works).

See Condition.

CONDITION SUBSEQUENT

See Condition.

CONSIDERATION

An act or promise, of legal value, done or given by the promisee in respect of and at the time of the promise made to him. Consideration may consist of anything having legal value (eg payment of money, the performance of work or services, delivery of goods, a conveyance of land, a forbearance to sue, etc). In *Currie v Misa* (1875) it was said that 'valuable consideration may consist either in some right, interest, profit or benefit accruing to the one party or in some forbearance, detriment, loss or responsibility given, suffered or undertaken by the other'. The law will not enforce a promise in the absence of consideration unless the promise is in the form of a deed.

See Contract.

CONTRACT

Derived from *con-tractum* and denoting agreement (ie the drawing together of two minds to form a common intention). Agreement is the primary but not the only element necessary to create a legally binding contract. In addition to a valid offer and unconditional acceptance, there must be form or consideration, capacity to contract, genuineness of consent and legality of objects.

The law imposes upon a party to a contract a legal obligation to perform or observe the terms of the contract and gives to the other party a right to enforce fulfilment or to claim damages for non-fulfilment (ie breach of contract). As a general rule contractual rights and liabilities affect only the parties to the contract and a person who is not a party can neither sue nor be sued on the contract. There are, however, a number of exceptions to this rule, the most important being in the field of Agency and Land Law where covenants may bind future owners of land.

Contracts may be either simple (parol) contracts or formal (specialty) contracts. A simple contract may be in writing (not under seal), oral or implied from the conduct of the parties. A formal or specialty contract is one made by deed which must be signed, sealed and delivered by the person or persons executing it. Promises made by deed are binding by virtue of the form which they take and do not need to be supported by consideration. Another important distinction is that under the Limitation Act 1939 an action on a specialty contract must be brought within twelve years of the date of the breach, whereas for a simple contract the limitation period is six years.

Some contracts (eg of guarantee or for the sale or other disposition of land) must be in writing to be enforceable, but it is clearly highly desirable to set down the terms of complex building contracts in written form so as to avoid future disputes.

A contract which has been entered into because of the special skill or knowledge of one of the parties is known as a personal contract. An employer's contract with his architect falls into this category and the effect is to prevent the architect from delegating his responsibilities to a third person without the consent of the employer. Similarly, a contract with a contractor could be personal if entered into because of the contractor's special experience of the work in question.

Where the contract calls for the entire fulfilment of the promise made by one party as a condition precedent to call for fulfilment of any part of the promise of the other party, it is described as an entire contract. The strict application of this principle to building contracts could cause considerable hardship to a contractor who for some minor infringement might be unable to recover any payment for the work done. In recognition of this the courts have developed the doctrine of substantial completion by which the contractor, if he can show that he has substantially performed his obligations, is entitled to payment less the value of any deficiencies.

There are certain kinds of contracts in which the law imposes upon one or both of the parties a duty to disclose material facts (ie facts which if known to the other party would influence the giving or withholding of his agreement). These are called contracts *uberrimae fidei* (ie of the utmost good faith) and include contracts of insurance, contracts between partners, principal and agent, solicitor and client, trustee and beneficiary.

Building contracts may be broadly divided into Fixed Price Contracts and Cost Reimbursement Contracts. The Fixed Price contracts may be either Lump Sum contracts, in which the contract sum is predetermined and stated in the agreement, or Measurement contracts, in which the contract sum is ascertained on completion by measuring the work done and valuing on the basis of an agreed

Schedule of Rates. Lump Sum and Measurement contracts may be further designated Firm Price contracts where no provision is made for the adjustment of price variations; where such provision is made they are also designated Fluctuating Price contracts. Cost Reimbursement contracts differ in that, in lieu of unit rates, the contract price is ascertained on the basis of the prime cost of labour, materials and plant plus a percentage or fixed fee for overhead charges and profit. A variant of this is the Target Cost contract in which a preliminary target cost is estimated and on completion the difference between the target and the actual prime cost is apportioned between the employer and the contractor in an agreed way.

Where the contractor is responsible for both design and construction the contract is referred to as a Package Deal or Turnkey contract. Employers who have a continuing building programme can obtain the advantages which stem from continuity of work by arranging Serial Contracts which are based on offers obtained for a firm programme of specific jobs of a similar nature and planned for execution over a stipulated period. Similar advantages can be obtained in the case of maintenance and repair work by the adoption of Term contracts for which Standing Offers are invited to do all work of a specified type over a prescribed period or term, the work to be valued on a measurement or cost reimbursement basis.

See Agreement. Law Report: *Appleby v Myers* (1867); Legislation: Unfair Contract Terms Act 1977.

CONTRACT DOCUMENTS

The documents which can be identified as containing the terms of a concluded contractual agreement between the parties which was made in, or reduced to, or recorded in writing. The standard forms of building and civil engineering contract make specific reference to the documents which it is intended should form part of the contract, and the building form makes provision for their signing by the parties to acknowledge (without enhancing) their status. They usually include the Articles of Agreement and Conditions, Drawings, Bills of Quantities and Specification.

In construing the intentions of the parties the contract documents are considered as a whole, although it may be provided that one of the documents is to prevail in the event of inconsistencies. Thus the JCT Conditions of Contract give priority to the printed word whereas the ICE Conditions of Contract provide that the various documents are to be taken as mutually explanatory and that any ambiguities are to be explained and adjusted by the employer.

In general, documents used in the negotiations leading up to the formation of the contract, but which are not incorporated in the contract, will have no effect unless their omission was due to a common mistake or to a mistake by one of the parties known to the other party — when the remedy of rectification may be available. Thus in *Davis Contractors v Fareham UDC* (1956) the contractor was unable to rely on a letter making his tender subject to the availability of adequate labour, in that although the letter was attached to his tender it was not subsequently incorporated in the contract.

CONTRACTOR

One who contracts to carry out and complete construction works in return for a financial consideration. The contractor is responsible for the planning of the work and for the acquisition and deployment of resources on site to achieve the completion of the project. Subject to any term to the contrary he is liable to the employer for the defaults of his sub-contractors, including those nominated by the employer through his architect or engineer.

An alternative term used for lesser works is 'builder', which has been judicially interpreted as 'a person who builds upon his own land or that of another for profit' and could be applied to an individual self-employed tradesman. Building contractors and civil engineering contractors, as the terms imply, are respectively concerned with works of building or civil engineering construction; these functions are not, however, exclusive.

CONTRACT SUM

The sum of money which the employer agrees to pay the contractor as considera-tion for carrying out and completing the contract works. The conditions of contract usually provide for the adjustment of the contract sum in a prescribed way in respect of changes in the contractor's obligations (eg variations to the quality or quantity of the works).

COPYRIGHT

An exclusive right relating to the reproduction or performance of literary or artistic works. In the absence of express provision to the contrary, the copyright in all plans prepared by him remains with the architect. In addition the architect has a copyright in the artistic design of the building itself but not in the con-structional techniques adopted in its erection. Thus where an extension is carried out in the style of an existing building the architect is technically entitled to a reasonable licence fee. However, once the work has started the Copyright Act 1911 limits the issue of an injunction stopping its continuance.

See Law Reports: *Meikle v Maufe* (1941); *Blair v Osborne & Tompkins* (1971).

CORPORATION

Corporations are legal entities created by charter or statute for a great variety of purposes appertaining to the advancement of religious, educational and commercial objectives. They may be regarded as artificial persons which are able to own property more or less for ever, irrespective of changes in their membership. A corporation may be a corporation sole, composed of one office holder such as a bishop, or (the most common example) a corporation aggregate, composed of more than one person, such as a company. The powers of a corporation created by statute are limited to those expressly stated in the Act of Parliament or those which by necessary implication are included in the express powers. On the other hand, a corporation created by Royal Charter can do everything that an ordinary individual can do.

A corporation can only act through its agents and any contract into which it enters must not only be within the powers of the corporation but also within the express or implied authority of the agent. However, an agent such as a local government architect may have ostensible or implied authority by virtue of his position.

Local authorities and the public corporations which operate the nationalised industries are corporate bodies whose constitution and powers derive directly or indirectly from statute. Any act which falls outside the prescribed limits is said to be *ultra vires,* and unless it can be shown that the act was reasonably incidental to the carrying out of a statutory function would entitle anyone adversely affected to a remedy. Trading corporations may owe their existence to charter or special statute but in the great majority of cases are incorporated under the Companies Acts.

CORRUPTION

The offering or giving of any gift, secret commission or other consideration for the purpose of inducing an agent to do or forbear from doing some act to the detriment of his principal's interests. Any such secret dealings between the architect and the contractor would amount to a fraud on the employer entitling him to dismiss the architect and recover any sum which had been paid to the architect as a bribe. The employer may additionally rescind the contract and claim for any loss suffered as damages from the contractor or architect. The court will presume that the bribe influenced the agent's actions without enquiring into the actual consequences. The offering or giving of bribes is also a criminal offence under the Prevention of Corruption Acts 1889 to 1906.

COST REIMBURSEMENT CONTRACT

See Contract.

COSTS

The expense of litigation or arbitration incurred by a party thereto. A successful party normally obtains an order or award requiring the unsuccessful party to pay his 'party and party' costs. The making of such an award or order (or an award or order for payment of less than the full proportion of party and party costs or of costs on another basis) is a matter within the discretion of the judge or arbitrator. This discretion must be exercised judicially and not whimsically, and an award or order other than a normal one would have to be supported by reasons. The actual calculation of the amount of costs to be paid (if this cannot be agreed) is done by a High Court taxing master. The total liability of a party is called 'solicitor and own client' costs, and a party can normally expect to obtain an award of between sixty-five and eighty per cent of that full total on a 'party and party' taxation. There are also various rules applicable to costs; thus under Section 47 of the County Courts Act 1959, if an action founded on contract or tort is referred to the High Court and could have been commenced in the County Court, and the plaintiff recovers less than £400, he is normally entitled only to County Court costs.

A defendant who is sued for damages may make payment into court of a sum of money and will not be liable for costs if the sum eventually awarded as damages is less than that paid in. Although there are no similar provisions in the case of arbitrations, a party against whom a money claim is made may make a sealed offer (an offer notified to the other side and put in a sealed envelope which is placed in the possession of the arbitrator) or an open offer on the terms that it will not be disclosed to the arbitrator until he has made his substantive award and before considering the question of costs. The sealed offer is likewise not opened by the arbitrator until after his substantive finding. In such cases the arbitrator should usually treat the offer as equivalent in effect to a payment into court.

COUNTER-CLAIM

A cross-claim brought by the defendant against the plaintiff in respect of or arising out of or connected with the same matter as the plaintiff's claim. Thus where A has a claim of any kind against B and brings an action to enforce such claim, and B has a cross-claim of any kind against A which by law he is entitled to raise and have disposed of in the action brought by A, then B is said to have a right to set-off and counter-claim.

COUNTER-OFFER

A response to an offer suggesting new or modified terms may constitute a counter-offer which on acceptance by the other party forms a binding contract. Thus in *Davies Shopfitters Ltd v William Old* (1969) the contractor's order to a

34

nominated sub-contractor introduced a new term (that the sub-contractor was not to be entitled to payment until the main contractor was himself paid), and this was held to be a counter-offer which had been accepted by the action of the sub-contractor in starting work.

See Formation.

COURTS

The Courts fall into six categories: Magistrates' Courts, Circuit Courts, County Courts, High Court, Court of Appeal (Criminal and Civil Divisions) and the House of Lords. The Magistrates' Courts, Circuit Courts and County Courts are known as 'inferior' Courts in that they are subject to the control of the High Court. Those not subject to this control are known as 'superior' courts. The Magistrates' Courts, also known as Courts of Summary Jurisdiction, have a mainly criminal jurisdiction and deal with the minor crimes of society. They are usually composed of three lay persons known as Justices of the Peace and are advised by a legally qualified clerk. The County Courts are wholly concerned with civil jurisdiction (ie the resolution of disputes between people and organisations as opposed to disputes between the State and people and organisations). Their main jurisdiction relates to such matters as landlord and tenant and disputes in contract and tort where the amount of money at stake does not (currently — ie 1980) exceed £2000. It is also the centre from which the Small Claims Court operates.

The High Court is divided into three — the Family Division, the Chancery Division and the Queen's Bench Division. Disputes relating to the construction industry are normally referred to the Queen's Bench Division. Subject to any right of trial by jury, the court can order that the matter shall be tried by an Official Referee, a circuit judge who specialises in cases involving an investigation of detailed and complicated issues.

The Court of Appeal sits in two divisions, the Civil Division, which hears appeals on civil matters from the High Court and the County Courts, and the Criminal Division, which replaced the Court of Criminal Appeal in 1966 and hears appeals on criminal matters against conviction and sentence. In the Civil Division the judges are the Master of the Rolls and the Lords Justices of Appeal sitting three in a court.

The 'court' of the House of Lords (properly called the Appellate Committee) usually consists of five senior judges who are also members of the House of Lords; technically they are called 'Lords of Appeal in ordinary'. Permission to appeal to the House of Lords is granted by the Court of Appeal or by the Appeal Committee of the House of Lords (usually three Lords of Appeal) only (1) in cases where large sums are at stake or where some important principle is involved, and (2) where the party losing in the Court of Appeal appears to have a good arguable case.

Decided cases form an important source of law and create binding precidents, a judge being bound to follow the *ratio decidendi* (ie the principle(s) supporting the decision) of a previous case decided by a court of equivalent or higher status. Thus, for instance, a principle established many years ago by the House of Lords may not be overthrown by the Court of Appeal unless it can be shown that the circumstances are not precisely the same as those which surrounded the earlier decision. The House of Lords is alone in not being bound by its previous decisions. Also principles established by decided cases may be modified or changed by statute.

COVENANT

A promise contained in a deed. The rules surrounding covenants are very complicated and each case needs separate consideration. For example, a negative restrictive covenant contained in a transfer of land (eg a promise given by the purchaser of the land to the vendor who retains adjacent land, that he will not use the land for, say, the erection of a factory) can usually be enforced by the successors of the vendor against subsequent purchasers or assignees. On the other hand a positive restrictive covenant (eg that the purchaser will repair and maintain the fencing) is much harder to enforce if the original parties to the transaction have disposed of their interests.

See Contract.

CRIMINAL LIABILITY

Liability for an act of commission or omission prejudicial to the community at large, being an act prohibited by common law or statute and, if committed, punishable by fine or imprisonment.

CUSTOM

A custom or trade usage is a generally accepted way of doing something or an established mode of conduct in a particular trade or profession. It will be treated as an implied term of a contract if there is evidence to show that the custom is notorious (ie so well known in the trade or profession that the parties must have intended it to apply), that it is reasonable and certain in its application, and that it is not contrary to law.

Customs will only be implied if there are no express provisions excluding them or if they do not contradict any necessarily implied terms. Thus in *Townsend (Builders) Ltd v Cinema News* (1959), where there was an express term in the contract requiring the contractor to comply with the byelaws, it was held that the contractor was liable to the employer for bringing the work into conformity with the byelaws notwithstanding the custom that it was the architect's responsibility to obtain the necessary approvals.

Customs do, of course, change and judgements in past cases may not necessarily provide an authority for proving the existence of a present custom. Nor do provisions in the standard forms of contract, although widely adopted, afford such evidence.

See Law Reports: *North v Bassett* (1892); *Gibbon v Pease* (1905).

DAMAGE

The expression 'loss or damage' is commonly used in provisions relating to the insurance of the works to indicate the effects of the specified risks to be covered by the insurance policy. In this context damage connotes the loss in value of the works caused by the occurrence of the insured contingency and is equivalent to the cost of restoring the works to its original condition.

The word may be used in a more general sense as, for example, in the ICE Conditions of Contract which places an obligation on the contractor to use every reasonable means of avoiding unnecessary damage to the highway. It may also be used to cover personal injury, and in some instances may also extend to financial loss.

See Damages.

DAMAGES

This is the term used to describe the award of financial compensation by a court arising from a breach of contract or from a tort. The amount awarded may constitute 'nominal' damages, indicating that although a right has been infringed no real loss has been suffered; or 'aggravated' damages which reflect the manner in which the wrong is inflicted as well as the wrong itself; or 'exemplary' damages (very rare) which not only compensate the plaintiff but are also designed to punish the defendant; or 'substantial' damages, which represent the actual loss suffered. In the latter case the measure of damages for breach of contract is the loss which flows naturally from such breach or which may reasonably be supposed to have been in the contemplation of the parties when they entered into the contract as being the probable outcome of the breach. The amount may be abated if the plaintiff has not taken all reasonable steps to mitigate his loss; conversely if reasonable steps have, through no fault of the plaintiff's, increased his loss, that increased loss might also be recoverable.

It is usual in building and engineering contracts to make provision for the recovery of damages by the employer if the contractor fails to complete the works by the original or any extended completion date. In order to avoid such damages being construed by the court as a penalty and set aside, they must be liquidated and ascertained (ie they should represent a genuine pre-estimate of the actual loss likely to be suffered as a result of the breach). The current law is as stated in the Court of Appeal decision in *Peak Construction (Liverpool) Ltd v McKinney Foundations Ltd* (1970), namely that liquidated damages provisions of a contract cannot be enforced if there has been delay due to the employer's default and either the extension of time clause does not make provision for such a delay or there has been a failure to extend the time. The importance of this is that liquidated damages — in so far as they are a genuine pre-estimate of losses likely to be sustained — may include for exceptional losses which the employer may be unable to recover as ordinary common law damages.

See Law Reports: *Victoria Laundry v Newman* (1949); *Wraight v PH & T (Holdings) Ltd* (1968); *Radford v De Froberville* (1977).

DAYWORK

A method of valuing work on the basis of prime cost (ie actual cost to the contractor) of labour, materials and plant, plus an agreed percentage to cover overhead charges and profit. The prime cost of labour is obtained by taking the total hours worked by each class of operative and by multiplying such totals by the appropriate all-in hourly wage rate. In the case of materials the prime cost is the invoiced amount after making any necessary adjustments in respect of trade and cash discounts. Usually it is agreed that the employer is to have the benefit of any trade discounts and of cash discounts exceeding five per cent. Plant is usually charged at agreed hourly rates inclusive of fuel and operator's wages.

The various categories of prime cost are defined in the publication *Definition of Prime Cost of Daywork carried out under a Building Contract*, issued jointly by the Royal Institution of Chartered Surveyors and the National Federation of Building Trades Employers.

DEED

See Contract.

DEEMED

This is a word which was used, frequently loosely and unnecessarily, in the pre-1980 JCT Conditions of Contract to denote that something might be validly assumed or judged to be as stated. The worst example was in Clause 12 which provided that the quality and quantity of the work was 'deemed' to be as set out in the Contract Bills which were 'deemed' to have been prepared in accordance with the principles of the Standard Method of Measurement of Building Works and that any errors or omissions were to be corrected and 'deemed' to be variations. These provisions have been incorporated in the 1980 edition at Clause 2.2 without a single use of the offending word.

The continued usage of 'deemed' in Clause 4.2 (previously Clause 2(2)) is however correct, namely that whether or not an instruction is in fact empowered by the Conditions of Contract it shall be judged (ie deemed) to be so empowered if the contractor complies with the instruction after being told in writing by the architect which provision of the contract empowers the issue of such instructions and, by implication, whether the architect be right or wrong in his judgement.

DEFECT

An imperfection in material or work which renders it unfit for the intended use. It may be a patent defect which is immediately obvious or a latent defect which is only revealed with the passage of time. The contractor has an implied liability for both patent and latent defects, although, as shown by *Gloucestershire County Council v Richardson* (1968), his liability in respect of latent defects may be excluded if the employer requires him to enter into a contract with a supplier on terms which severely restrict his recourse against such supplier.

It is usual in building contracts to give the architect express powers to order the removal or re-execution of defective work before practical completion, and subsequently to impose an obligation on the contractor to make good any defects which appear during the stipulated defects liability period. The latter obligation (namely to do work as opposed to paying the cost of rectification as part of a claim for damages) would be restricted to defects due to materials or workmanship not in accordance with the contract or to frost occurring before practical completion. It should be noted that the expression 'defects liability period' is peculiarly ill-named since it corresponds in no way with the period during which the contractor remains liable for defects.

See Limitations.

DEFENDANT

This is the term used to describe the person or company against whom proceedings in the High Court are brought; the party bringing them is called the plaintiff. In arbitration these parties are usually termed respondent and claimant respectively, although an arbitrator may in appropriate circumstances direct that a party commencing arbitration proceedings shall appear in the reference as the respondent.

DELAY

Delay is the subject of concern in construction contracts when there is a failure on the part of the contractor to proceed with reasonable diligence or to perform a task at the rate or by the time necessary to meet a contractual obligation.

A distinction must be drawn between delayed progress and delayed completion. It is usual to provide express remedies, on the one hand, for the recovery by the employer of liquidated damages for unjustifiably delayed completion, and on the other hand, for the grant to the contractor of an extension of time for delay in the progress of the works caused by exceptionally inclement weather or for delay on the part of the architect in issuing necessary instructions, drawings, details and the like. As will be obvious, these matters are outside the control of the contractor and may well cause a delay in the progress of the works which is likely to result in delayed completion. In the latter case provision may also be made in the contract for the recovery by the contractor of loss and/or expense consequent upon the delay caused by the architect, but in the absence of such a provision the contractor's remedy (if any) will be in damages for breach of contract on the grounds of interference by the employer's agent.

In the absence of express provisions relating to dates for commencement and completion, the concept of 'reasonable time' would be invoked; by which is meant 'reasonable in all the circumstances' and involves a consideration of essentially factual, rather than legal, matters.

See Law Reports: *Duncanson v Scottish County Investment Co* (1915); *J Henshaw & Sons v Rochdale Corporation* (1944).

DEROGATION

See Abrogation.

DESIGN

Design has been described as the exercise of those functions that use scientific principles, technical information and imagination to define a project capable of meeting specified requirements with economy and efficiency. The term may be related to the aesthetic qualities of the building, to the functional suitability of the overall concept and layout for the intended use, or to the technical adequacy of the constituent materials and construction.

Traditionally the architect is liable for the overall design of a building and is not entitled to delegate his responsibility without the employer's consent. In *Moresk Cleaners Ltd v Hicks* (1966) it was held that if the architect was not able to design the work himself he should: (1) tell the client that the work was not in his field, or (2) ask the client to employ a specialist, or (3) pay a specialist out of his own pocket and retain the responsibility. However, with the increasing complexity of buildings, more and more of the design must be carried out by consultants or specialist sub-contractors, and this is recognised by the RIBA Conditions of Engagement which restrict the architect's liability in this regard to the direction and integration of the specialists' work.

Where any part of the design work is entrusted to another it is important for both the building owner and the architect to establish (where the RIBA Conditions of Engagement do not apply) precisely what is the ambit of the architect's responsibility to the building owner. Does it, for example, embrace the work of the 'other' or not? If this matter is not dealt with specifically, a fruitful area for future disputes is being prepared — an area in which the custom of passing specialists charges through the architect, combined with the habit of some architects of charging their fees on the total cost of the works, provides a good basis from which the building owner may argue that the architect has an overall responsibility to him for the total design.

A design may be expressed graphically — in the form of dimensioned and annotated drawings and sketches; in writing — in the form of specifications, bills of quantities, schedules, letters and other documents; orally — by direct instructions; physically — in the form of models, samples, templates, etc; numerically — in the form of punched paper or magnetic tape or other computer-input medium; or in any combination of these ways.

In the absence of express provision the architect owns the copyright in both the plan and the design of a building and the client may not without the architect's permission repeat the design of other buildings. It is traditional in building works for the architect to depict and describe the finished product and its constituent parts and materials and to entrust to the contractor the task of combining the parts and constructing the whole. This will not, however, in itself relieve the contractor from joint responsibility for the technical adequacy of the finished work.

See Law Report: *Greaves & Co Contractors v Baynham Meikle & Partners* (1975).

DETAILS

A somewhat imprecise term used to describe the larger scale drawings or sections of a drawing which show selected parts of the construction in greater detail than is possible on the general arrangement drawings. The term may also embrace schedules and written instructions which are issued during the progress of the contract for the purpose of amplifying the contract documents.

DETERMINATION

The bringing to an end of a contract where one of the parties elects either to exercise a contractual right or to treat a fundamental breach by the other as a repudiation.

The JCT Conditions of Contract give the employer and the contractor a right to determine the contractor's employment in specified circumstances. This right is expressed to be without prejudice to any other rights and remedies the employer or the contractor (as the case may be) may have, and is therefore additional to and not in substitution of the common law right to rescind a contract for what is often called a fundamental breach. However, not all of the breaches named in the contract as giving rise to the contractual right are sufficiently serious to give rise to the right at common law to treat a contract as repudiated. Also it should be noted that the contractual right is to determine the employment of the contractor and not the contract as a whole. Thus the terms of the contract which govern the rights of the parties after such determination will continue in effect.

See Forfeiture. Law Reports: *Gloucestershire County Council v Richardson* (1968).

DILIGENCE

A failure by the contractor to proceed 'regularly and diligently with the works' may result in the determination of his employment under the JCT Conditions of Contract. In the ICE Conditions of Contract the term 'due expedition' is employed to similar effect.

Whether or not, in general terms, the contractor is proceeding diligently or with due expedition is a matter to be decided in the particular circumstances of a contract, but one test would be to ascertain whether the rate of progress is consistent with the contractor's obligation to complete by the agreed date or, in the absence of such agreement, within a reasonable time. Whether or not the powers of determination *(vide* JCT conditions) and forfeiture *(vide* ICE conditions) are exercisable may depend upon the more limited test of what (if anything) has happened in the period after the serving of the preliminary notice which the relevant conditions call for.

See Delay, Reasonable Progress.

DIMINUTION

See Set-Off.

DIRECT LOSS

This term is used in the JCT Conditions of Contract to qualify the extent of the loss which the contractor can recover in respect of the disruptive effect of disturbance of the regular progress of the works caused by stipulated contingencies. It may be that the types of losses envisaged are similar to those claimable at common law as ordinary damages, although there is a contrary view which argues that since the JCT Conditions of Contract distinguish between 'loss and expense' (eg Clauses 24 and 26) and 'loss and damage' (eg Clauses 27 and 28), there must be a difference between the two, and if so, presumably 'loss and damage' is the wider and the one which corresponds to ordinary damages. If this is right then it would follow that 'loss and expense' should be construed so as to produce a lesser basis of recovery.

Whichever be the right approach, ordinary damages were defined in *Hadley v Baxendale* (1854) as either those which arise naturally as a normal consequence of the breach or those which may reasonably be supposed to have been in the contemplation of the parties when they made the contract as being the probable outcome of the breach. Thus unusual or extraordinary losses would only be recoverable on proof of special circumstances known or reasonably within the contemplation of the parties at the date the contract was made.

See Damages.

DIRECTION

See Instruction.

DISCLAIMER

A technical term denoting the power given to trustees in bankruptcy, and liquidators, to reject onerous contracts which are uncompleted at the time of the bankruptcy or liquidation. The power must be exercised within twelve months of appointment or upon application by an interested party within twenty-eight days or such longer period as the court may allow. The effect is to end the contract and terminate all the rights and interests of the insolvent party in the contract, leaving the other party to prove for damages.

The right to disclaim is given by statute to the liquidator or trustees to be exercised in the interests of the general body of creditors. It is difficult to avoid the conclusion that Parliament intended the trustee or liquidator to have an effective choice (ie to continue the contract or to disclaim). If that be so, it must be extremely doubtful whether the parties can effectively agree to exclude that right and in effect prefer one creditor to the general body. Therefore the automatic determination (on liquidation or bankruptcy) clauses must be regarded as of problematical effect, and any party considering relying on them would be well advised to seek another ground for action. This caveat probably does not apply in the case of a receiver or manager.

See Adoption.

DISCOVERY OF DOCUMENTS

In legal proceedings a court, including an arbitrator, may at its own instigation, or upon the request of either party, order the disclosure of all documents containing information which may either directly or indirectly enable a party to advance his own case or to answer that of the other party. This process is described in legal jargon as 'discovery' and the disclosure usually takes the form of a list of all pertinent documents, whether privileged or not, in the possession of the party; discovery is followed by inspection of the non-privileged documents.

In High Court proceedings discovery is automatic and must take place within fourteen days after service of the last pleading. However, the court has power to dispense with discovery in whole or in part and to extend the time necessary for discovery — this latter being an essential step in most building disputes.

DISQUALIFICATION

The act of depriving a certifier or an arbitrator of the qualifications necessary for the performance of his functions. The more common reasons for disqualification are fraud, collusion with one of the parties or other failure to act impartially as between them, and concealment of any unusual interest which is likely to influence judgement.

Usually a certifier would not be disqualified if his interest were disclosed at the time the agreement was made, but in relation to arbitrators the Arbitration Act 1950 provides that an arbitrator's authority may be revoked if his relation to one of the parties is such that he might not be capable of impartiality even though the other party knew this, or ought to have known it, at the time the agreement was entered into. Thus whilst the employer's architect would not be disqualified from acting as certifier, he might well, by virtue of his relationship with the employer, be disqualified from acting as arbitrator even though named as such in the agreement. The relevant provision empowering the court is Section 24; it is doubtful if a single application to disqualify has been made under the 1950 Act.

DISTURBANCE

The term is usually encountered in relation to the regular progress of construction works, and in the particular sense of disruption of such progress arising from causes outside the contractor's control, or which could not reasonably have been foreseen by him when entering into the contract.

See Delay, Interference.

EASEMENT

A right which the owner of property, known as the dominant tenement, enjoys over another property, known as the servient tenement. The right may be granted by the owner of the servient tenement or be acquired by prescription following long usage. The more common easements are rights of light, rights of support, private rights of way and rights of drainage across the property of another.

There are a number of other rights which are similar to but which do not constitute easements; for instance a profit à prendre is a right to take something from the land of another and a licence is a private right to go on the land of another.

There are also quasi-easements (referred to in the ICE Conditions of Contract) which consist of various rights such as local customary rights and certain habitual rights over different parts of land in common ownership.

ELEMENTAL BILL OF QUANTITIES

See Bill of Quantities

EMPLOYER

This is the term used in building and civil engineering contracts to describe the contracting party for whose benefit the work is carried out. This usage must be distinguished from the more general one, meaning employer of labour. Where the work is to an existing building the term 'building owner' is sometimes used as an alternative. The analogous term in the GC/Works/1 Conditions of Contract is 'the Authority' and means the person designated in the Abstract of Particulars to act on behalf of the employing department.

ENGINEER

A general term which requires a qualifying prefix to give it a precise meaning. The types of engineers most usually concerned with construction works include civil engineers — who are skilled in works of public utility such as roads, railways, bridges, canals, docks and harbours; structural engineers — who form a relatively new profession and undertake the design of the structural elements of buildings and other constructions; mechanical engineers — who are responsible for the design and construction of mechanical equipment such as lifts and escalators; electrical engineers — who are concerned with the production and transmission of electrical energy and with the design and installation of electrical services; and heating and ventilating engineers — who design and install their systems in buildings.

All the foregoing engineers may be commercially involved in contracting or sub-contracting and offering both design and construction services or they may be employed in the public service or engaged in private practice as independent consultants. Unlike 'architect' there is no restriction on the use of the title 'engineer', although practising engineers are usually members of an appropriate professional body which lays down levels of competence, codes of conduct and scales of fees.

The ICE Conditions of Contract use the term 'engineer' to describe the person responsible for the design and supervision of the works, and they further provide for the appointment of an engineer's representative to assist the engineer in the carrying out of his duties. Engineer's representatives are commonly referred to as 'resident engineers' and may have restricted powers similar to those of a clerk of works or be given considerable delegated powers to act on behalf of the engineer. The ICE Conditions of Contract give greater powers to the engineer to dictate the method of working than is accorded to the architect under the JCT Conditions of Contract and they also envisage that the more important temporary works may be designed by the engineer.

The GC/Works/1 Conditions of Contract may be used for either building or civil engineering works, and accordingly the term 'Superintending Officer' is used to describe the person responsible for design and supervision, whether such person is an architect, engineer or other professional.

ENTIRE CONTRACT

See Contract.

ESSENCE

A contractual obligation is said to be of the essence of the contract where its performance by one party is expressed to be a condition precedent to the right to call for the performance of any part of the obligation of the other party. Thus, if payment is expressly made dependent upon completion by a stipulated date, then time is of the essence and the employer will be released from his obligation to pay the contract sum if the contractor fails to complete on time. However, it is unusual for time to be of the essence in building contracts and it cannot be so if there is provision for the payment of liquidated damages for late completion. In such a case it is clear that the parties had contemplated the possibility that completion might not be on time and had made specific provision to deal with such eventuality.

See Law Report: *United Scientific Holdings Ltd v Burnley Council* (1977).

ESTABLISHMENT CHARGES

See Overheads.

ESTIMATE

A forecast of some quantifiable value such as, and most commonly, the probable price or cost to the employer or contractor of construction works. Estimates are made by the employer's professional advisers at various stages in the design process in order to predict the amount of an acceptable tender.

The accuracy of such estimates will depend upon the amount of design information available. They range from early preliminary estimates — based on such parameters of the proposed building as units of accommodation to be provided, gross floor area or cubic capacity — to the more detailed estimates, based, when the design has been developed, on the measured quantities of the individual items of work which make up the whole. As the object is to determine the price to the employer, such estimates are usually based on analyses of past tenders received for similar buildings, adjusted to take into account differences in price levels and design parameters.

Following the decision in the case of *Nelson v Spooner* (1861) it has been held that if an architect prepares plans and drawings and from them gives an estimate of the probable cost, he may not be able to recover his fees if the lowest tender is so far in excess of the estimate that the employer is unable to afford to proceed with the project. However, if the employer can achieve substantially his objectives whilst making some reductions in the work, he should give the architect the opportunity of altering his plans in order to obtain an acceptable tender.

Estimates made by contractors are attempts to determine as accurately as possible the actual expenditure on construction resources needed to complete the proposed building. They are therefore based so far as possible on records of the contractor's own site costs and the informed opinion of his estimator.

A distinction needs to be made between the contractor's estimate, as a factual statement of predicted costs, and his tender, which reflects the firm's policy and takes into account other factors such as the prevailing market conditions and the keenness of the contractor to obtain the contract. The addition to (or subtraction from) the estimated cost made to arrive at the tender is sometimes known as the 'mark-up' and the principles by which this adjustment is determined as 'bidding theory'. It would appear that at law there is no distinction deriving simply from the nomenclature used and in the case of *Crowshaw v Pritchard* (1899) it was held that a tender submitted on paper headed 'estimate' was a binding offer and that if, as the contractor maintained, there was a custom to the contrary it was bad at law and not enforceable.

See Quotation, Tender.

ESTOPPEL

A rule of evidence precluding a person from denying the truth of that which he has previously asserted, or has at least allowed to go uncorrected or unchallenged. This arises principally in relation to unambiguous statements in deeds which are taken as binding and not admitting of contradictory proof, and to representations which the other party has acted upon to his detriment. It is necessary however that the representation should be positive and intended to be (and be) acted upon. Thus, in *Royston UDC v Royston Builders Ltd* (1961) the employer was not estopped from relying on a clause in the contract which limited the payment of increased costs to listed materials merely because claims for the increased costs of other materials had been paid in interim certificates.

EXCEPTED RISKS

A term used in both the JCT and ICE Conditions of Contract to describe the various types of risks which are excluded from the Contractor's general liability to indemnify the employer in respect of loss or damage and against which he need not insure.

The risks covered in the JCT Conditions of Contract are restricted to the hazards associated with radio-active substances and processes and pressure waves caused by aircraft or other aerial devices. The ICE Conditions of Contract cover, in addition, riot, war, invasion, civil war, rebellion, revolution, insurrection and military or usurped power.

The term should be distinguished from that of 'accepted risks' used in the GC/Works/1 Conditions of Contract to describe a somewhat different set of hazards.

EXECUTION

In its legal sense the term is used to indicate that everything necessary to the bringing into existence of a contract has been carried out. Thus a deed is executed when it has been signed, sealed and delivered.

The word is also used in construction contracts in its general sense denoting the carrying out and completing of works by the contractor.

See Formation.

EX GRATIA

Literally 'from favour', the term is used to refer to a payment made for alleged loss or damage for which there is no pre-existing liability on the part of the payer. Such payments are entirely discretionary and are sometimes referred to as 'sympathy' or 'hardship' payments.

EXPERT WITNESS

A witness selected by a party to legal or arbitral proceedings to give evidence on the basis of his special knowledge of the subject matter of the dispute. The main difference between an expert witness and an ordinary witness is that the former is not limited to statements of fact but is entitled, if asked, to give his opinion on matters in which he is expert.

Prior to the trial or hearing, the expert witness is usually required to provide a report setting out his opinions on the matters in issue which fall within his special competence. The expert's report must be served on the other side as a condition of leave to call his evidence.

EXPRESS TERM

An express term or condition is one which is specifically stated in the contract documents and which will override any directly conflicting terms which would otherwise be implied in relation to the same matter.

See Implied Term.

EXTENSION OF TIME

Where a contract provides for the payment of liquidated damages to the employer for failure by the contractor to complete by a certain date, it is necessary to have a parallel provision for extending the time in the event of delays being occasioned by causes outside the contractor's control or caused by the actions of the employer or his agents. In the absence of such a provision, delays caused by the employer or his agents would nullify the original completion date and lose the employer the right to claim liquidated damages.

An employer may be entitled to ordinary damages if the contractor does not complete within a reasonable time, but these may be hard, if not impossible, to prove and anyway would not normally include any extraordinary losses which might legitimately have been included in the liquidated sum.

See Delay. Law Reports: *Miller v London County Council* (1934); *Amalgamated Building Contractors v Waltham Holy Cross UDC* (1952).

EXTRA WORK

Work which is not expressly or impliedly included in the work for which the tendered sum is payable. Where the contractor quotes a lump sum based on drawings and/or a specification, there is an implied obligation to do all indispensably necessary work at no extra cost, whether or not such work is shown on the drawings or described in the specification. However, where the scope of the work included in the price purports to be precisely defined, as in a bill of quantities, any work in excess of the measured quantities, in so far as it is properly done in response to a valid instruction and not rendered necessary by any default of the contractor, would be treated as a variation.

If extra work is completely outside the scope of, and quite unrelated to, the original contract work then it may well not be a variation and may become the subject of an implied new contract and of a *quantum meruit* payment. However, if both parties treat it as a variation it might well be difficult for either party subsequently to contend that it was to be treated as the subject of a separate contract.

See Law Reports: *Molloy v Liebe* (1910); *Brodie v Cardiff Corporation* (1919).

FAIR VALUATION

See Quantum Meruit.

FAIR WAGES

It is common for contracts for public works and buildings to contain conditions which require the contractor to observe and fulfil the obligations upon contractors specified in the Fair Wages Resolution passed by the House of Commons on 14 October 1946. This Resolution requires those engaged on central and local government contracts to give fair treatment to their employees in relation to wages, conditions and union membership, to display a copy of the resolution in every work-place associated with the contract works, and to ensure the observance of the resolution by any sub-contractors.

There appear to be no recorded instances of the clause giving rise to litigation and the provision is probably superfluous in the present climate of industrial relationships.

FIDIC

The acronym for *'Fédération Internationale Des Ingénieurs-Conseils'*, the leading organisation of an international group of organisations which sponsors a standard form of contract for use internationally for works of civil engineering construction.

The FIDIC Conditions of Contract are modelled very closely on the ICE standard form but a notable difference is the provision, in Part II of the document, of an *aide-mémoire* for the drafting of 'conditions of particular application' — being terms dealing with matters of substance and importance which can only be completed with due regard to the particular local circumstances. Part III of the document provides conditions of particular application to dredging and land reclamation work.

See ICE Conditions of Contract.

FIDUCIARY

A relationship of trust.

FIRM PRICE CONTRACT

See Contract.

FIXED PRICE CONTRACT

See Contract.

FLUCTUATING PRICE CONTRACT

See Contract.

FLUCTUATION OF PRICE

See Formula Price Adjustment, Variation of Price.

FORCE MAJEURE

As with the concept 'act of God', *force majeure* is pertinent to construction contracts when used to describe circumstances which, should they occur, will relieve the contractor from his obligation to complete the works by the contract date for completion.

It is a term taken from the *Code Napoléon* and does not appear to have a precise interpretation in English usage. However, it can be presumed to have a wider connotation than 'act of God' and to cover both man-made and naturally occurring circumstances. In the case of *Hackney BC v Dore* (1922) it was held that it must have a physical or material nature, and that threatened action giving rise to a fear — which in turn caused a breach of contract — could not be construed as *force majeure*.

It seems likely that the national emergency which resulted in the 'three-day working week' of 1973/74 constituted *force majeure*. More recently a number of contractors have prayed the provision in aid in cases where work on sites has been brought to a complete halt by industrial action which was essentially political rather than social. It has yet to be decided whether this is in fact *force majeure*.

FORFEITURE

Strictly this is the right of one party to determine a contract by reason of the other having repudiated it by a breach of a fundamental term. This is a right which exists apart from any express provision of the contract relating to forfeiture or determination.

Clause 63 of the ICE Conditions of Contract is sub-titled 'forfeiture' and recites a number of acts or omissions of the contractor (eg insolvency; abandonment of the works; failure to commence or proceed diligently with the works) which will entitle the employer to expel the contractor from the site '... without thereby avoiding the contract or releasing the contractor from any of his obligations or liabilities under the contract ...'.

Both the GC/Works/1 and JCT Conditions of Contract contain similar provisions which they summarise as 'determination', a word used by the ICE Conditions of Contract only in relation to the respective rights of the parties in the event of the works not being completed within twenty-eight days of the outbreak of war. The distinguishing feature of the JCT Conditions of Contract, however, is the express provision of terms relating to the contractor's powers of determination of his own employment under the contract (eg in the event of the employer obstructing the issue of or failing to pay on the architect's certificate, or if the works are suspended by the employer for a specified time).

Even contracts which are forfeited under the general law (ie by operation of implied rather than by express terms) do not come to an end and the provisions of the contract will continue to govern the rights and obligations of the parties in so far as they remain relevant.

See Law Report: *Hounslow BC v Twickenham Garden Development Ltd* (1971).

FORMAL CONTRACT

See Contract.

FORMATION

The act of creating a binding contract, the essential elements of which are a definite offer and an unconditional acceptance of such offer. It should be noted that where it can be presumed from the circumstances in which an offer is made that the parties contemplated that the postal service might be used as a means of communicating the acceptance, such acceptance is effective, and the contract is formed, as soon as it is posted. Conversely, the revocation of an offer is not effective until it is received (before, of course, the offer has been accepted) by the party to whom the offer was first made.

See Execution.

FORMULA PRICE ADJUSTMENT

A specific method of calculating the amount to be added to or deducted from the contract sum by way of allowance for increases or decreases in the costs of labour and materials occurring during the currency of the contract. A contract admitting such adjustment is commonly known as a fluctuating price contract as opposed to a fixed price contract.

All the common standard forms of contract contain adoptive clauses to cover such adjustment if a fluctuating price contract is intended. Broadly speaking, the price adjustment may be made in two ways: either by ascertainment of the actual fluctuation in price to the contractor of labour and material resources allocated to the contract in question, or by adoption of a formula under which the fluctuations are calculated theoretically by reference to statistical indices and as a result of which the financial adjustment may be more or less than that actually experienced by the contractor in relation to the contract in question.

The indices referred to in the ICE Conditions of Contract (which contain a supplementary clause relating to contract price fluctuations) are those compiled by the Department of the Environment and published by HMSO in the Monthly Bulletin of Construction Indices (Civil Engineering Works). The method of applying these indices is sometimes referred to as the Baxter Formula.

In the case of the JCT Conditions of Contract the general reference is to the National Economic Development Office Price Adjustment Formula for Building Contracts, with specific mention being made of Formula Rules which are further defined as 'the formula rules current at the Date of Tender issued for use with this clause by the Joint Contracts Tribunal for the Standard Form of Building Contract ...'. In turn the Formula Rules define the effective indices as those compiled by the Department of the Environment and published by HMSO in the *Monthly Bulletin of Construction Indices (Building and Ancillary Civil Engineering Works and Specialist Engineering Installations).*

The provision for price fluctuations in the GC/Works/1 Conditions of Contract is known as the 'Variation of Price supplementary condition'.

FOSSILS

'The remains of animals and plants belonging to past ages and found embedded in the strata of the earth' — *Shorter Oxford English Dictionary.* It is usual to declare in construction contracts that any such objects found on the site are the property of the employer.

See Antiquities.

FRAUD

Fraud is a type of deceit (a tort) and involves leading a party into damage by wilfully or recklessly causing him to believe and act upon a falsehood. Where fraud occurs in connection with construction contracts it usually takes the form of fraudulent misrepresentation — the making of a false statement of material fact which is intended to induce a contract and which is uttered, to quote the words of Lord Hershal in the leading case of *Derry v Peek* (1889), 'knowingly, without belief in its truth, or recklessly, careless of whether it be true or false'. Carelessness cannot, in the absence of dishonesty, be fraudulent, but there is a degree of recklessness which may be shown to be dishonest.

There must be damage consequent upon a fraud before an action will lie and such damage must be shown to have been incurred as a direct result of acting upon the fraudulent misrepresentation. A third party claiming as a consequence of a fraud between two other parties will have no cause of action. Conversely, no party can be excused from the commission of a fraud on the grounds that the action was that of a servant or agent. In the words of Lord Westbury: 'All persons directly concerned in the commission of a fraud are to be treated as principals' — *Cullen v Thompson's Trustees* (1862).

Failure to keep a promise is not necessarily fraud, nor can a mere statement of opinion be construed as a fraudulent misrepresentation. On the other hand a statement which is literally true but which, deliberately and with intent to mislead, omits some material fact is a falsehood and a cause of action if the other elements of fraud are present.

A fraudulent statement need not be in writing to be actionable, unless it is of the nature of a guarantee. The use of fraud to induce a contract or to influence its terms may result in rescission or may give rise to an action for damages for breach.

See Law Reports: *Pearson v Dublin Corporation* (1907); *Larkins v Chelmer Holdings Pty* (1965) (Aus).

FRAUDULENT MISREPRESENTATION

See Fraud, Misrepresentation.

FRUSTRATION

Agreements which are rendered void by certain circumstances outside the direct control of the contracting parties are said to have been frustrated and the resolution of such contracts will be at the discretion of the court under the Law Reform (Frustrated Contracts) Act 1943. Only a supervening event far outside the contemplation of the parties and rendering the venture wholly different in nature can result in frustration. As construction is an intrinsically risky business, such events are rare.

Even if a party contracts to do something which proves to be impossible, he will be liable in damages for his failure unless the impossibility is so fundamental (ie 'contrary to the laws of nature') that the contract is rendered void for want of consideration. The impracticability of, or difficulty in executing, constructional work will not excuse a failure to perform. Thus Blackburn J. in the case of *Taylor v Caldwell* (1863): 'Where there is a positive contract to do a thing, not in itself unlawful, the contractor must perform it or pay damages for not doing it, although in consequence of unforeseen accidents, the performance of his contract has become unexpectedly burdensome, or even impossible.'

Acts of God, Government edicts or devastating fires or floods may well be the cause of frustration, although in the latter events only the destruction of the site of the works — thus thwarting absolutely the original intention — would prompt such an outcome. The commonly used standard forms of contract provide for determination in the event of war, and such provision would appear to pre-empt frustration and the exercise of the court's discretion under the Act of 1943.

The consequence of frustration is the automatic discharge of both parties from their obligations, the contract being avoided. Where a party deliberately delays performance with the object of frustrating a contract he will have no remedy under the doctrine of frustration. In the case of a personal contract, the death of the personality will result in frustration and the avoidance of the contract from the moment of death. Any rights secured up to such time will, however, accrue to the deceased's estate.

The judgement in the case of *Davis Contractors v Fareham UDC* (1956) contained a definition of frustration: 'Frustration occurs whenever the law recognises that without default of either party a contractual obligation has become incapable of being performed because the circumstances in which performance is called for would render it as being radically different from that which was undertaken by the contract.' Lord Radcliffe went on to say, '... it is not hardship or inconvenience or material loss itself which calls the principle of frustration into play. There must be as well such a change in the significance of the obligation that the thing undertaken would, if performed, be a different thing from that contracted for.'

See Law Reports: *Metropolitan Water Board v Dick, Kerr & Co* (1918); *Kursell v Timber Operators & Contractors* (1927).

GARNISHEE ORDER

An order of the High Court requiring a third party, who in the ordinary course of business owes money to a debtor in a court action, to pay the amount in judgement direct to the creditor.

Thus A, who has been given judgement for a debt owing by B, may apply for a Garnishee Order enabling him to obtain payment of the judgement debt direct from C, who is a normal debtor of B.

See Law Report: *Dunlop & Ranken v Hendall Steel Structures* (1957).

GENERAL LIEN

See Lien.

GOODS

Merchandise, the commodities of commerce which may be bought and sold, are commonly called goods. The only area of the English Law of Contract which is comprehensively codified is that relating to goods. The statutory provisions relating to this area of law have been consolidated in the Sale of Goods Act 1979.

Construction contracts, being agreements for the execution and completion of work — that is for both the supply and the incorporation of goods into a complex end-product — do not fall within the sphere of the Sale of Goods Act. It is the case, however, that contractors and sub-contractors will in the normal course of their business engage in many sale of goods transactions, the purpose of which will be on the one hand to transfer the title in goods from the seller to the buyer, and on the other hand to ensure that such goods answer to the description of them used in the contract of sale. Although both these aspects of a transaction — proprietary and functional — give rise to disputes, it is perhaps the latter which occurs most frequently in relation to construction contracts.

In any contract for construction work there will, in the absence of specific provisions, be implied obligations to use goods which are fit for their purpose and of good quality. There will be similar terms implied in any contract for the sale of goods to the contractor, but in such case warranties of fitness for purpose and of adequate quality will be implied by the Sale of Goods Act.

The question as to whether a contract is for the sale of goods or for work and materials is one to be decided with regard to the circumstances of each case. The judges in the action *Lee v Griffin* (1861) were unanimous that when 'the contract is such that a chattel is ultimately to be delivered ... the cause of action is goods sold and delivered'. This particular case concerned two sets of false teeth made and supplied by a dentist and held to be a sale of goods. However, when the installation of the manufactured article is part of the contract and where such installation is an important element of the transaction — as in the case, say, of lift equipment — the contract will most likely be one for work and materials and not for the sale of goods.

It is to be noted that clauses which seek to retain for the supplier some degree of physical control over the goods supplied are becoming common. The purpose of the control is to give the supplier an effective sanction to enforce payment, and a popular method is by creating a trust. Such clauses may work (see eg *Aluminium Industrie Vaassen B V v Romalpa Aluminium Ltd* (1976)) and must be considered very carefully before being used or agreed to.

See Materials. Law Reports: *G H Myers & Co v Brent Cross Service Co* (1934); *Samuels v Davis* (1943); *Gloucestershire County Council v Richardson* (1968); *Young & Marten Ltd v McManus Childs Ltd* (1968).

GUARANTEE

A contract under which one party, the surety, undertakes in the event of the default of a second party over the payment of a debt to, or the performance of some act in favour of, a third party, to be answerable to the third party for such default.

A guarantee is essentially a collateral contract for it cannot exist in the absence of the agreement of which performance is being guaranteed. To be enforceable it must be in writing, and if not under seal must be supported by consideration and formally accepted by the party to whom it is offered. In relation to construction contracts, guarantees need to be very carefully expressed so as to ensure that the surety is undertaking to guarantee due performance of those of the contractor's obligations which are crucial to the employer, the nature of which is frequently complex.

The provision of sureties is sometimes a condition precedent of construction contracts in the local government sector, and in such cases it is common to require a bond, being an agreement under seal, rather than a simple contract of guarantee. This is because of the complications surrounding the matter of consideration for a guarantee, which usually exists between the surety and the potential defaulter rather than directly to support the obligation to protect the third party. Thus the insurance company which gives the guarantee or bond will usually be paid by the contractor and not by the building owner. The amount of that payment will of course be reflected in the contractor's price and thus emanates from the building owner; but such an indirect route is probably not sufficient to support a contract between insurer and building owner in the absence of a deed; hence the requirement of a bond.

It follows from the foregoing that the consideration for a guarantee need not be expressed in the suretyship agreement itself and need not take the form of a benefit to the surety. For example, an adequate consideration would be an undertaking by the third party to abstain from enforcing his legal rights against the second, defaulting, party.

The three-cornered arrangement of guarantee and principal contracts makes the obligations of suretyship somewhat onerous and the law has evolved to afford some measure of protection for guarantors against acts which may prejudice their position. For example, concealment of material facts relating to, or the alteration of, material terms within the principal contract may vitiate the guarantee, as may the failure of a party to the principal contract to preserve some security to which the surety is entitled.

The suretyship will end with the fulfilment of the obligations guaranteed, providing such performance cannot be set aside by legal process. The matter may be further complicated by an open guarantee given by the directors of the contracting firm, or (if the latter is a subsidiary) by the parent company, to the insurance company as bondsmen.

See Law Report: *General Surety v Francis Parker* (1977).

HAND-OVER

The process of delivering up the site and the works to the employer upon completion of a construction contract. Considering the importance of this event it receives scant attention in the commonly available standard forms of contract.

The ICE Conditions of Contract only refer directly to the delivering up of the works in the associated standard form of tender; otherwise the conditions refer to the event indirectly through the provisions relating to completion. The JCT Conditions of Contract also use the term 'completion' but refer directly to the 'possession' of any part or parts in advance of practical completion of the works as a whole. The GC/Works/1 Conditions of Contract do have a specific term requiring the contractor to deliver up the site and the works.

HIRE

Simple hire is distinguished from hire-purchase by the absence of the option to purchase, and although such agreements may provide for the extension of the hire period in return for a purely nominal rent, thus giving the hirer possession of the goods for their entire useful life, property in the goods remains with the owner.

Clause 53 of the ICE Conditions of Contract is designed to ensure that an employer will not, in the event of forfeiture, be denied the use of the defaulting contractor's plant because, being hired rather than owned, property in such plant resides in the owner and not in the contractor. It does this by requiring any 'agreement for hire' (which term is expressly declared to exclude hire-purchase) entered into by the contractor to contain a condition permitting assignment of the hire contract to the employer. The effectiveness of this clause depends upon the contractor complying with it. If he simply does not bother, the owner is left with a claim for breach of contract against the contractor, rather than a right to use the plant. The JCT Conditions of Contract contain no such provision and, as with hire-purchase, an employer under a determined building contract will almost always have no rights in relation to hired plant.

HIRE-PURCHASE

A contract between an owner and a hirer under which goods being and remaining the property of the owner are held on bailment (which in this case amounts to a rental arrangement) by the hirer who will also have an option to purchase. The hirer cannot pass any title to the goods. Hire-purchase agreements are not subject to the provisions of the Sale of Goods Act 1893 for there is no contract of sale unless the option to purchase has been exercised. In the event of bankruptcy of the hirer the owner can recover the goods.

In relation to construction contracts the main implication of hire-purchase is that contract conditions which purport to give the employer a lien on, the right to retain, or the right to make use of, the contractor's plant and equipment, in the event of some failure on the part of the contractor to proceed with the contract works, may be rendered ineffective by virtue of the legal ownership of the plant and equipment residing in someone other than the contractor.

The Hire Purchase Act 1965 was designed mainly to protect the interests of personal domestic hirers. The act does not apply when the hirer is a corporate body nor when the hire purchase price exceeds a stated sum (currently £2000).

HOSTILITIES

See Excepted Risks.

ICE CONDITIONS OF CONTRACT

A standard form of contract for work of civil engineering construction sponsored jointly by the Institution of Civil Engineers, the Association of Consulting Engineers and the Federation of Civil Engineering Contractors within the United Kingdom. It is the most commonly used form of contract for civil engineering works.

The full and correct title of the document is: *Conditions of Contract and Forms of Tender, Agreement and Bond for Use in Connection with Works of Civil Engineering Construction.* The work is currently in its fifth edition; this was published in June 1973 and contains significant changes from the earlier editions. A permanent joint committee keeps the use of the document under review and will receive suggestions for amendment at the Institution of Civil Engineers, 1 Great George Street, London SW1P 3AA.

A contract under the ICE Conditions requires the use of a specification, drawings and bills of quantities. The Conditions are intended to give rise to a 'measure and value' as distinct from a 'lump sum' contract and draw a specific distinction between the 'tender total', which is the financial basis for acceptance, and the 'contract price', which is the sum to be paid on completion of the contract. The resulting agreements will nevertheless be entire contracts under which the obligation to complete is, subject to the doctrines of substantial performance and impossibility, an absolute one.

See FIDIC.

ILLEGALITY

An act contrary to the law as laid down by Parliament or the courts and as expressed in parliamentary statutes or cases decided by the courts. One cannot contract to perform an illegal act and an agreement which purports to provide otherwise will be void and unenforceable whether or not the illegal nature of the proposed act was known to one or more of the contracting parties.

The courts do not look at knowledge — hence the maxim *'in pari delicto potior est conditio defendentis'* — 'when the guilt is equal the position of the defendant is the stronger'.

A contract which is legal at its commencement may be rendered illegal by some subsequent legislation or decision of the courts and will consequently be frustrated and the parties discharged from any further obligation to comply with its terms. The commission of an illegal act within the performance of an otherwise legal contract (eg the deliberate execution of work in contravention of the Building Regulations) can found no rights of either party. Where a plaintiff cannot establish his case without demonstrating the illegality of some act under the contract, he cannot succeed in contract; but if he has been deceived by fraudulent misrepresentation into believing in the legality of the act, a remedy might lie in damages for fraud.

See Law Reports: *Metropolitan Water Board v Dick, Kerr & Co* (1918); *F W Clifford Ltd v Garth* (1956); *Townsend Ltd v Cinema News* (1959).

IMPLIED TERM

Even an unnatural degree of attention to detail would be unlikely to result in a set of written terms which, except for the simplest of agreements, would be comprehensive beyond question. Consequently, whilst the best evidence of the terms of a contract will be their inclusion in a written memorandum of agreement, there remain a number of matters which, in the absence of written terms, will be implied either because they are notoriously matters of particular trade usage or because the contract would otherwise be unworkable. Terms will not be implied where the effect is merely to make the agreement more or less favourable to one party, neither will a term be implied that is at odds with the written agreement.

In construction contracts which do not specify in detail the materials and workmanship required, there will be an implied term that such shall be of a reasonable standard having regard to the subject matter of the contract and that the completed work shall be fit for its ostensible purpose. Similarly, in the absence of a specific date for completion, a reasonable contract period will be implied.

See Law Report: *Bacal (Midland) Ltd v Northampton Development Corporation* (1976). Legislation: Supply of Goods (Implied Terms) Act 1973.

IMPOSSIBILITY

An undertaking to perform an impossibility renders a contract void for want of consideration; but for this to be the consequence the impossibility must fall within one of three limiting definitions. The impossibility may arise from a matter of illegality, the act contracted for being legally forbidden; it may be absolutely impossible, being contrary to the laws of nature; or it may be impossible by virtue of the subject matter of the contract, without the knowledge of the contracting parties, being non-existent at the time the agreement is made.

Impossibility may occur subsequent to the making of the contract and in such case performance is not necessarily excused and the party failing to perform will be liable for damages. There are two exceptions to this rule, the first when the subject matter of the contract ceases to exist and the second where the contract is a personal one only capable of performance by a specific party who dies or is otherwise totally incapacitated.

It should be noted that there is no generally implied undertaking that an architect or engineer's design is possible of completion and that in principle a contractor must complete an impracticable design in the best way he can or pay damages. In this connection impossibility must not be confused with impracticability. A contractor having to complete an impracticable design is unlikely to have any redress against the employer, nor would the employer necessarily have to pay for the cost of executing amendments ordered by the architect in an attempt to ameliorate the problem.

An equally rare and related occurrence in construction contracts is frustration.

See Law Report: *Thorn v London Corporation* (1876).

INCLEMENT WEATHER

The influence of the weather on the efficiency with which many construction operations can be carried out is a self-evident phenomenon. Whilst the risk of interference with regular progress of construction works by inclement weather is usually placed quite firmly with the contractor, presumably on the grounds that he is as well equipped as the next man to obtain forecasts of the weather likely to be experienced during the course and in the location of a proposed contract, it is also a common provision of building contracts that the contractor shall be entitled to claim relief from the contractual consequences of any delay in completion which is directly attributable to exceptionally inclement weather.

It is not usual for any attempt to be made within a contract to define what is normal weather so that the degree of inclemency can subsequently be identified. This must always be a matter for agreement in particular circumstances. It should be noted that the relief offered is usually limited to the granting of extra time for the completion of the works and does not extend to the reimbursement of loss or expense consequent upon the inclement weather itself.

The ICE Conditions of Contract specifically exclude weather conditions or conditions due to weather conditions from the class of 'adverse physical conditions' which might entitle a contractor to recover consequent loss or expense. The 1980 editions of the JCT Conditions of Contract employ the phrase 'exceptionally adverse weather conditions' in place of the phrase 'exceptionally inclement weather' used in earlier editions.

INCORPORATION

The fact of inclusion of a specific document in an agreement. It is not necessary to provide to a contracting party all documents subsidiary to the main conditions or even to list such documents in a specific appendix. It is sufficient for such subsidiary documents to be referred to in the contract conditions with, in appropriate cases, a clear indication of any limitation on the pertinence of the subsidiary document to the contract in question.

There is a presumption that despite any points of agreement made in the negotiations leading to a written contract the only terms which will subsequently be held to govern the behaviour of the parties under the contract will be those incorporated in the written memorandum of agreement. Notorious trade usages of certain effect and which are reasonable in operation and not contrary to law may, in the absence of express incorporation, be held to form implied terms of either written or oral agreements. Conversely, such trade usages may be expressly excluded by agreement.

See Trade Usage. Law Reports: *Davis Contractors Ltd v Fareham UDC* (1956); *Royston UDC v Royston Builders Ltd* (1961).

INDEMNITY

An undertaking by one party to hold another party free from pecuniary loss which might result from one or a number of specified occurrences and the quantum of which may be incalculable at the time the indemnity is given. An indemnity can be entered into orally and will be binding without specific acceptance by the indemnified, unlike a guarantee, which must be in writing and which must be formally accepted by the party to whom it is offered.

Indemnities are frequently incorporated in construction contracts. Usually, but not exclusively, they are given by contractors in favour of employers with the object of protecting the employer from pecuniary loss consequent upon claims made on him by third parties alleging injury as a direct consequence of the con- tract works. For such indemnities to be effective the indemnifier must be able to meet the financial consequences of any claim and consequently it is usual to require the indemnifier to take out insurance, in the joint names of the indemnifier and of the indemnified, to cover the occurrences referred to in the indemnity; this does of course require some evaluation to be made of the probable extent of any loss.

It must be emphasised that as a contract of insurance is designed to protect a party from specific pecuniary loss, such party cannot recover both under the indemnity and under the contract of insurance. This is because once the insurer has paid against the loss, the indemnified loss has been removed and there is nothing for an indemnity claim to bite upon. As a consequence it is important to ensure either that the insurance associated with indemnities is taken out in the joint names of the parties to the indemnity contract (so as to exclude the operation of the doctrine of subrogation), or that it includes '... a provision whereby in the event of any claim in respect of which the Contractor would be entitled to receive indemnity under the policy being brought or made against the Employer the insurer will indemnify the Employer against such claims and any costs charges and expenses in respect thereof' – Clause 23(2) of the ICE Conditions of Contract. Such a provision is known as a 'cross-indemnity' or 'principal's clause'.

It should also be noted that the courts have decided that indemnity clauses should not be construed so as to protect a party against his own negligence unless such protection was expressly intended. Where a third party, having suffered some injury, can establish the joint responsibility of both parties to an indemnity agreement, the Law Reform (Miscellaneous Provisions) Act 1934 may be invoked to obtain an apportionment of the claim for the purposes of contribution, regardless of the provisions of the indemnity agreement.

A cause of action over an indemnity can arise only when the indemnified loss has been established; this means that the limitation period relevant to the indemnity will only then begin to run.

See Law Reports: *Alderslade v Hendon Laundry Ltd* (1945); *Walters v Whessoe Ltd and Shell Ltd* (1960); *AMF International Ltd v Magnet Bowling Ltd and G P Trentham Ltd* (1968); *County & District Properties v Jenner & Ors* (1976); *Smith v South Wales Switchgear Co* (1978).

INDEPENDENT CONTRACTOR

The distinction between an independent contractor and an employee, or servant, is an important one on several counts, not least of which is the high degree of statutory control of contracts of employment and the relative rights and duties of employers and employees which exist despite the express terms of any contract between them. The distinction is perhaps more easily recognised in practice than it is defined, but the independent contractor will usually be under an agreement which relates to a specific act, or related series of acts, to be undertaken within a specific period of time, rather than one which relates to continuing responsibilities.

The test of control may also assist in making the distinction, thus: 'A servant is a person subject to the command of his master as to the manner in which he shall do his work' – Bramwell, L J in the case *Yewens v Hokes* (1880); but there will be many cases where this test is difficult to apply. A better test may be whether or not the individual is, in the words of Lord Denning giving judgement in *Bank voor Handel en Scheepvaart NV v Slatford* (1953), 'part and parcel of the organisation'.

See Law Reports: *Humberstone v Northern Timber Mills* (1949); *Ready Mixed Concrete Ltd v Minister of Pensions and National Insurance* (1968).

INJUNCTION

An equitable remedy granted at the discretion of the courts to secure the discontinuance of some injurious action whether arising under contract or tort. In general an injunction will not be granted where damages would provide an appropriate remedy. For this reason it is the common remedy for acts of nuisance. An injunction is the converse of an order for specific performance, but whilst an arbitrator can order specific performance an injunction can be granted only by a court of law.

INJURY

Construction is a physically hazardous business and contracts usually contain conditions which place responsibility for injury to persons or to property on the contractor and which attempt to indemnify the employer from claims for such injuries resulting from the contract works. An injury need not be physical; for example, noise or smells generated by construction works may be injurious to the enjoyment of adjacent property or even to mental health. The constructional activity may itself injuriously affect the value of an adjacent business by deterring would-be customers.

The courts will generally take a reasonable view of constructional work, accepting that landowners or occupiers have a right to build, albeit that the right is always circumscribed by the obligation to do it in such a way as not to cause unreasonable interference with the rights of others, which in this context probably means that all steps which can reasonably be taken to minimise the interference must be taken. The usual remedy for injury is damages, but in so far as the reputed injury takes the form of nuisance it will be more usual to seek an injuction to restrain its continuance.

See Trespass. Law Report: *Rylands v Fletcher* (1868).

INNOCENT MISREPRESENTATION

See Misrepresentation.

INSOLVENCY

A financial condition which results when a company is unable to meet its debts as and when they fall due. An individual in the same condition is said to be bankrupt. The law relating to the insolvency of companies is governed by the Companies Acts and that relating to the insolvency of individuals by the Bankruptcy Act 1914; although the practical effect of both statutes is similar, there are important differences in detail. However, the Insolvency Act 1976 heralds the formulation of a comprehensive insolvency system covering both bankruptcy and winding-up procedures. Although this Act currently deals only with non-controversial technical and procedural amendments, it is significant in that it encompasses both branches of insolvency law.

An insolvent company is usually wound up involuntarily on the petition of a creditor; this type of winding-up is controlled by the courts. The most usual alternative form of winding-up is where the creditors form or elect a committee and themselves control the process consequent upon a resolution by the company to wind up. Once a court order is made, or the committee established, a liquidator is appointed — often an accountant, and if the size of the collapse justifies it, a member of a firm specialising in such work. Such liquidator will often have been the receiver or manager prior to the order or resolution.

The liquidator seeks to bring all the assets of the company, including its current contracts, into his custody and control. Insolvency does not by itself cause the termination of a contract or constitute a breach of it, since the liquidator may obtain leave to continue the business of the insolvent party in an attempt to minimise the final deficit. Furthermore, it is doubtful whether an attempt to tie an automatic determination of contractual rights (other than those guaranteed by a lease) to the making of a winding-up order will be effective. This is because the purpose of the insolvency procedures is to benefit the creditors as a body; and in the absence of specific statutory authority it is questionable whether one creditor can help himself to what may be a valuable right (eg to finish the contract) at what is, effectively, the expense of the other creditors.

In relation to construction contracts the timing of the formal state of insolvency may be of material significance to anyone trading with the insolvent party.

See Liquidation.

INSPECTION OF DOCUMENTS

See Discovery of Documents.

INSPECTION OF WORKS

See Inspector.

INSPECTOR

It is common for standard forms of contract to provide for the inspection of the contract works in course of construction by a representative of the employer and for the issue of instructions to the contractor consequent upon such inspection. Although the powers of inspection are normally vested in the employer's principal agent (ie the architect, superintending officer or engineer), the JCT Conditions of Contract specifically provide that the employer shall be entitled to appoint a clerk of works whose duty is to act solely as inspector on behalf of the employer but under the directions of the architect. The ICE Conditions of Contract permit the engineer to delegate to his representative his powers of inspection and in turn any number of assistants may be appointed to help him with these duties. The GC/Works/1 Conditions of Contract provide that a clerk of works or resident engineer may be appointed to exercise such powers of the superintending officer as that officer may give notice of to the contractor.

In the absence of contractual provisions for inspection, or in the event of any inspection being made inadequately, the contractor will not be relieved of any of his responsibilities to construct and complete, and any defective work will have to be remedied when discovered. Thus the function of an inspector is, by identifying potential causes of defect at their source, to mitigate any subsequent disturbance of the quiet enjoyment of the completed works (ie damage to the employer) and to reduce the cost to the contractor of rectification.

Inspectors are also appointed by local authorities and other bodies for the purpose of ensuring that statutory requirements and regulations are complied with. It was held in *Anns v Merton London Borough Council* (1977) — it following earlier cases — that local authorities had a general duty to exercise a proper degree of skill and care when inspecting buildings for the purpose of the Building Regulations.

See Law Reports: *Jameson v Simon* (1899); *Cotton v Wallis* (1955).

INSTALMENT

See Interim Payment.

INSTRUCTIONS

It is usual for the conditions of construction contracts to contain provision for the giving of instructions, orders or directions by or on behalf of the employer to the contractor. Such instructions may be necessary to resolve some uncertainty resulting either from the contract documents or from some eventuality associated with the site or physical conditions affecting the execution of the works.

Most construction contracts provide that the employer may by instruction vary the contract works. In all such cases some formal evidence of the instruction will be required and conditions governing the issue and receipt of instructions are a common feature of standard forms of construction contract. The more important of such provisions are the identification of persons having the authority to issue instructions — and the definition of any matters outside the scope of such authority, and the procedure for responding to oral instructions — and for the written confirmation of the same.

The power to issue instructions is usually limited to the employer's main agent (ie the architect, superintending officer or engineer). Subsidiary functionaries such as clerks of works and engineer's representatives and assistants may be given limited powers to instruct subject to immediate confirmation in writing by the principal agent. The onus of recording oral instructions in writing is usually placed upon the contractor, who is required to submit the written record for formal approval.

See Variation. Law Reports: *Kirk & Kirk v Croydon Corporation* (1956); *Neodox v Swinton & Pendlebury BC* (1958).

INSTRUMENT

A term sometimes applied to a document of legal significance (ie by means of which a person does a legal act — transfers land, undertakes obligations etc), which document may be used formally as evidence of the state of affairs existing between parties, or to communicate the exercise of some authority vested in the originator of the document (eg a certificate or a notice).

INSURANCE

The common contraction of the expression 'contract of insurance', being a contract under which one party (the insurer) undertakes in consideration for a payment (called a premium) by another party (the insured) to pay a sum of money to the insured upon the occurrence of some prescribed event which causes the insured a pecuniary loss, usually by reason of damage to persons or property. The amount of the premium is calculated by reference to the probability of the event occurring and to the anticipated extent of the loss. The terms of a contract of insurance are known as a policy.

Construction can be a physically hazardous activity, not only to those engaged in it but also to third parties adjacent to or visiting the site of the works and to associated property. Although it is usual under construction contracts to make the contractor responsible for any damage resulting from the works and for indemnifying the employer against resulting claims, it is also usual for the employer to insist that such indemnity be backed up by policies of insurance taken out by the contractor.

It will be clear that damages is a peculiarly inappropriate remedy for a breach of an undertaking to insure and that contract conditions relating to insurance should provide that in the event of failure by the appropriate party to provide evidence of having insured, usually by production of the policy of insurance and of premium receipts, the other party can himself insure the risk and set off the premium payments against any sums due from him to the defaulting party.

See Abrogation, Averaging.

INSURRECTION
See Excepted Risks.

INTEREST
Where a person in whom is vested powers of certification has a direct interest in the outcome of the certification process, then such interest will not disqualify the certifier if it was disclosed at the time the agreement was made. If it was not disclosed to a complainant then the courts may set aside the certifier's decision. The Arbitration Act 1950 provides, however, that even though an interest of a named or designated arbitrator — in an agreement to refer future disputes — has been disclosed, such fact shall not be a ground for refusing an application by either party to revoke the authority of the arbitrator or for an injunction to restrain him from proceeding with it on the grounds that he is or may be impartial.

INTEREST ON MONEY
Money invested or used for business purposes can earn income — sometimes described as interest and sometimes as return on capital. From this it follows that the withholding of monies due to a party either effectively denies that party the ability to invest such money (and hence to earn interest) or to use such money (and hence provide a return) and may result in that party having to borrow a sum equivalent to that due and to pay interest on the loan.

In the absence of express agreement, or of trade custom, interest is not recoverable under the common law in respect of simple debts. However, interest will be recoverable as an element of damages where money has been withheld by fraud, and also under the provisions of the Law Reform (Miscellaneous Provisions) Act 1934. Under this Act a court (including a court of arbitration) may, in proceedings for damages or for the recovery of a debt, include interest in its award. It should be noted that the discretion to include interest is a consequence of the legal proceedings and that it may only accrue from the time when a cause of action arose. The court has absolute discretion over the rate of interest to be applied, over the sum to which it will be applied and over the period in respect of which it can be charged. It is, however, almost invariably the case that the recovery will be less than from a commercial investment.

It is to be noted that the courts are slowly moving towards a recognition of the high cost of financing activities — as illustrated by the case of *Minter v Welsh Health Technical Services Organisation* (1980) where the JCT Conditions of Contract (pre-1980 edition) were construed as giving rise to the right to reimbursement of financing charges in certain circumstances.

INTERFERENCE

In the absence of express provisions to the contrary, an employer cannot interfere either with the contractor's freedom to occupy the site of the works or with his method of carrying out the works; to do so will be a prima facie breach of contract. To the extent that a contract provides for the variation of the works upon the instructions of the employer (or his architect or engineer), the mere issue of such instructions cannot be construed as interference; but the particular wording of the contract will determine whether or not the timing and incidence of an instruction to vary the works is such as to amount to a breach of contract which will entitle the contractor to damages or whether the timing and incidence falls within the contemplation of the contract.

Interference with the contractor's occupation of the site and with his method of working which stems from the presence on the site of invitees of the employer will provide no cause of action for breach of contract unless the presence of such third parties was not envisaged when the contract was entered into.

An employer who interferes with a person empowered by the contract to issue certificates in the exercise of such functions will lay himself open to an action for damages.

See Prevention. Law Reports: *Roberts v Bury Commissioners* (1870); *Acrow (Automation) Ltd v Rex Chainbelt Inc* (1971).

INTERIM CERTIFICATE

See Certificate

INTERIM PAYMENT

It is common for contracts for construction works expressly to provide that the contractor shall be entitled to payments on account as the work proceeds; the frequency of these advances or instalments is usually stipulated, as is the method of computing the amount due. The two most common methods are to calculate the sum from time to time by reference to the value of the work completed and of the materials delivered to the site for use in the works, or to agree sums, or proportions of the contract sum, which will be paid when the work reaches predetermined stages of completion, hence the expression stage-payments.

The existence of a provision for interim payments should not be allowed to obscure the fact that many construction contracts will be entire contracts, the instalments being distinguished from the final sum to which the rules relating to entire contracts will apply. In the absence of an express provision for interim payments such a term is unlikely to be implied by the courts. In the absence of express provisions to the contrary, the withholding of an isolated interim payment by an employer will not be interpreted as a repudiation of the contract.

Most standard forms of contract expressly define the rights and obligations of the parties in relation to interim payments.

See Interim Certificate. Law Report: *Hoenig v Isaacs* (1952).

INTERLOCUTORY

This adjective is used to describe the ancillary and the administrative hearings that take place on the way to a full hearing at arbitration or in the law courts. There will usually be an interlocutory hearing at the beginning of an arbitration to decide whether there are to be pleadings — and if so at what intervals of time, and whether the parties propose to be legally represented. Such a hearing is essentially administrative. There are also ancillary matters which may be the subject of interlocutory hearings, for instance, an application to the High Court by a defendant for security of costs to be given by a financially weak plaintiff company.

INVITATION TO TENDER

An invitation to tender is an invitation to treat, and not an offer to contract with any party submitting a tender. It is, however, the case that invitations to tender for construction contracts are usually so worded as to induce offers which are capable of immediate acceptance by the employer.

An invitation to submit tenders which expressly states that the lowest will be accepted will constitute a good offer which together with the acceptance enshrined in the lowest tender will result in a contract.

See Formation.

INVITATION TO TREAT

An offer to discuss the setting-up of a contract, or to negotiate with a view to entering into a contract, or to receive offers for goods available for sale — even though the price may be marked thereon — is an invitation to treat, and must be distinguished from the offer, which together with an acceptance forms one element of a simple contract.

See Formation. Law Report: *Fisher v Bell* (1961).

JCT

See Joint Contracts Tribunal.

JCT CONTRACT

A term used loosely to describe any one of the Standard Forms of Building Contract or Standard Forms of Sub-Contract issued by the Joint Contracts

Tribunal. There are three variants of the Standard Form of Building Contract, each of which is published in two editions, one for use by private individuals and organisations and one for use by local authorities and other public sector bodies of similar corporate status.

The three variants provide: (1) 'with quantities' conditions for lump-sum contracts (admitting of variations) in which bills of quantities are accorded contractual status and provide the definitive description of the quality and quantity of the work included in the contract sum; (2) 'with approximate quantities' conditions for measurement contracts which similarly incorporate bills of approximate quantities; and (3) 'without quantities' conditions for lump-sum contracts (admitting of variations) in which, instead of bills of quantities, the specification is accorded contractual status and provides the definitive description of the work to be included in the contract sum.

There are two variants of the Standard Form of Sub-Contract (referenced NSC/4 and NSC/4a respectively) which differ only in minor detail relating to the precise nature of the pre-contract procedures adopted by the parties.

As the name implies, the Standard Forms of Building Contract are intended to be used for building works as opposed to civil engineering works and for where the design is provided by the employer or the employer's agent; they are wholly unsuitable for design and build (ie 'package-deal') contracts. On the other hand, the Standard Forms of Sub-Contract do provide for the Nominated Sub-Contractor in appropriate cases to assume responsibility to the employer for the design of his work through the operation of a Standard Form of Collateral Agreement also published by the JCT (referenced NSC/2 and NSC/2a) together with a Standard Form of Nominated Sub-Contract tender (referenced NSC/1) and a Standard Form for Nomination of Sub-Contractor (referenced NSC/3).

As the standard forms are the product of negotiations amongst the various bodies participating in the Joint Contracts Tribunal, they naturally reflect the difficulties of obtaining agreement amongst parties whose interests are opposed.

JOINT CONTRACTS TRIBUNAL

A voluntary body whose primary function is to compile, issue and maintain various versions of a Standard Form of Building Contract, and, since 1980 of a Standard Form of Sub-Contract together with associated Forms of Tender, Collateral Agreement and Nomination. The organisations constituting the JCT are currently: Royal Institute of British Architects; National Federation of Building Trades Employers: Royal Institution of Chartered Surveyors; Association of County Councils; Association of Metropolitan Authorities; Association of District Councils; Greater London Council; Committee of Associations of Specialist Engineering Contractors; Federation of Associations of Specialists and Sub-Contractors; Association of Consulting Engineers; Scottish Building Contract Committee.

The term 'Tribunal' is a misnomer; the JCT is a committee of representatives of the constituent bodies and its decisions are unanimous expressions of the committee's views. It has no quasi-judicial or arbitral status, and although it issues 'practice notes' purporting to interpret provisions of its Standard Forms of Contract, such notes have no legal status and would not necessarily be accepted by a court of law. The JCT has a permanent secretariat provided in rotation by the constituent bodies. Documents issued by the JCT are currently published on its behalf by RIBA Publications Limited, 66 Portland Place, London W1N 4AD.

JOINT LIABILITY

See Liability.

JOINT TORTFEASOR

One of a number of persons jointly guilty of a tort. Under the Law Reform (Married Women and Tortfeasors) Act 1935 one tortfeasor who had been successfully sued could recover contribution from any other joint tortfeasor who was liable in respect of the same damage, the apportionment being made in such proportions as the court thought just and equitable.

   The Act provided a valuable remedy, but over the years it became generally accepted that the ambit of contribution (limited as it was to those liable in tort) was too narrow. Accordingly, the Civil Liability (Contribution) Act 1978 was passed which for practical purposes enacts that contribution can be obtained by a defendant from any one who has any civil liability in respect of the damage which is the subject of the claim against the defendant. It thus covers contribution from parties liable in contract or by statute, as well as in tort.

   The new Act applies to obligations assumed, debts falling due, or damage occurring, after 1 January 1979. So far as damage occurring before that date is concerned, the 1935 Act remains in force. The principle of assessment — namely what the court thinks just and equitable — remains the same.

JURISDICTION

The authority or power vested in a legally constituted court, whether of law or arbitration, or in some administrative body.

LABOUR

Frequently used as a collective noun to describe all the input to construction work which is not materials — hence 'labour and materials'. In such usage it embraces not only manual work but also management and the use of plant.

LATENT DEFECT

A latent defect is one the existence of which is established only when it can be shown to have induced some further damage which has become observable. It is a defect which at the time of its creation would be likely to go undetected even by an inspector exercising reasonable skill and care.

It is of the nature of construction work that faults develop in it over time and from a variety of causes, some of which may be quite unconnected with the original performance of the contractor. As a consequence, construction contracts usually limit the contractor's liability to return and remedy defects by his own labour, by prescribing a period of time (to follow completion of the contract works) during which notified defects must be made good by him. Upon the expiry of this period such liability ceases but he will remain liable in damages for the cost of the repair, and for any direct cost consequences, of any defects which can be shown to have resulted from some default on his part.

In the nature of things such defects (ie those giving rise to claims after the defects liability period) will be latent defects. In the absence of any contractual restriction or extension of this liability for damages it will be controlled by the Limitation Act 1939 which provides that the right to bring an action under a simple contract is extinguished six years after the date on which the cause of action accrued, and in the case of contracts under seal twelve years. The cause of action in contract (in the context of construction work) can for practical purposes be regarded as arising at the date of practical completion or the date of execution of the work, which ever is the later. However, in the context of construction work, the law has recently developed in such a way as to make the matter of liability in contract of appreciably less importance than other types of liability.

In the case of *Anns v Merton London Borough Council* (1977) it was held that a local authority carrying out its administrative functions was liable in tort to subsequent owners and occupiers for negligence. Being a liability in tort, the cause of action does not accrue (and therefore time does not start to run) until damage of the relevant type occurs. In Anns case damage of the relevant type was held to be actual or imminent damage to the health of the plaintiff.

Furthermore, the case of *Batty v Metropolitan Properties* (1978) made it clear that the law regards a builder as under a duty in tort to subsequent owners and occupiers to act carefully — and again the consequence of this is that time will not start to run until, at the earliest, the (negligent) defect is apparent.

The Defective Premises Act 1972 gives in respect of dwellings an additional ground of liability which applies to builders and developers alike and extends its benefit to anyone who acquires an interest in the dwelling. Any cause of action in respect of a breach of the duty imposed by this Act, (ie to see that the work is done in a workmanlike manner, with proper materials, so that the dwelling is fit for habitation) is deemed for the purpose of the Limitation Acts to have accrued at the time the dwelling was completed. However, the Act does not apply to houses which were sold with a National House-Building Guarantee.

See Defects Liability Period, Limitation.

LEGAL

Such as is required or permitted by law as distinct from equity. The sources of the law are Parliament and the courts and expressions of the law are contained in parliamentary statutes and cases decided by the courts. Equity exists side by side with statute and common law and provides a recourse to certain principles of justice which came into being in an effort by the Crown and the courts to supplement the existing case law and procedures and which are now enshrined in the law.

LIABILITY

Any obligation to do or to refrain from doing something and in respect of which one is answerable in law or equity. Apart from the joint and several liabilities which are either expressly or impliedly assumed by the parties to a construction contract, the activity of construction is a potential source of further liability both in relation to adjoining property and to persons unconnected with such contract. Furthermore, the common purpose of a contractor and an employer being the realisation of construction works, it is frequently found that a party asserting some injury resulting from the works will, whatever the immediate cause, proceed simultaneously against the contractor and the employer, alleging a separate liability on the part of each.

LICENCE

A formal commission from a constituted authority to do something. Whilst a contract may itself be perfectly legal it is frequently the case in construction contracts that the performance of some obligation under the contract may be illegal in the absence of some licence or other external authority relating to the subject of the obligation. For example, formal approval of construction designs will usually be required under the building regulations; also from time to time, usually arising from Government economic policy, it has been necessary to obtain a statutory licence to build at all.

The term is also used to refer to the granting by an employer of an implied permission for the contractor to enter on the employer's property for the purposes of executing the contract works.

LIEN

A possessory lien is a right to retain possession of property until a debt due to the party detaining such property is discharged. The property detained must have come legally and in the normal course of business into the possession of the party which claims the lien. A possessory lien does not confer the right of sale of the detained goods unless the parties have so agreed.

A particular lien is a right which arises in connection with the property which is the subject of the debt, the most common example being items left with a tradesman for repair and which need not be given up until the tradesman's charges have been paid. Similarly, drawings and specifications produced by an architect or engineer can be retained until the associated fees have been paid.

A general lien, which may arise in contract or by custom, is a right to detain property not only for debts incurred in connection with such property but also to set against other debts existing by way of trade between the parties. The businesses of accountancy, banking and stockbroking afford the best examples of this right. Liens are implied by law but similar rights can be created by express agreement. It is such rights, inaccurately termed liens, which are most frequently encountered in construction contracts and it is necessary to examine the terms of a contract in order to ascertain what rights over each other's property the parties have created.

See Seizure.

LIMITATION

The opportunity to enforce by action a right to a legal remedy under a contract is extinguished by the passage of time. This limitation of action is prescribed by Section 2 of the Limitation Act 1939 which provides that the right to bring an action on a simple contract is extinguished six years after the date on which a cause of action accrues; the corresponding period for a speciality contract (ie by deed and under seal) is twelve years. Notice of arbitration or the issue of a writ within the relevant period will secure the right.

Where the action is in respect of non-payment the cause will accrue from the date upon which the payment was due. When a breach giving rise to an action is a continuing one, the latest date of the continuing breach can be taken. Where there is fraudulent concealment (ie the covering up of work which was obviously bad), the period of limitation will not run until the fraud is discovered or until a reasonably diligent plaintiff should have discovered it.

Where the claim is in tort, the cause of action accrues and time starts to run when damage is suffered as a result of the breach. This may be appreciably later than the date of breach itself, as in the case of negligent foundations to a house not manifesting themselves until years after construction and during which time the house has been sold a number of times. In such a situation it will be clear that it is only the luckless buyer who is in possession when the foundations start to subside who suffers any damage.

See Law Reports: *Farr A E v The Admiralty* (1953); *Jas Archdale & Co v Comservices* (1954); *Clark v Woor* (1965); *County and District Properties v Jenner & Ors* (1976); *Anns v Merton* (1977); *Eames v East Herts Council* (1980).

LIQUIDATED DAMAGES

See Damages, Penalty.

LIQUIDATION

The process of winding up a company by bringing all its assets, including its current contracts, into the custody and control of a liquidator. The law relating to the liquidiation of companies is governed by the Companies Acts 1948-1980 and by the Insolvency Act 1976.

Liquidation by one of the contracting parties does not by itself cause the termination of a contract, or constitute a breach of it, since the liquidator may be able to continue the business of the company so far as may be necessary for its beneficial winding up. A party may, however, prove for damages immediately upon the liquidation of a company which has undertaken long term commitments; alternatively such party may apply for an order rescinding the contract and claim damages for non-performance.

See Adoption, Bankruptcy, Insolvency.

LIQUIDATOR

See Liquidation.

LITIGATION

A legal process resorted to in order to resolve a dispute which falls within the province of the law and which may arise under statute, contract or tort. Although litigation and arbitration are commonly used as mutually exclusive terms (or in contradistinction to each other) meaning, respectively, proceedings in court and proceedings before an arbitrator, it may be that arbitration should, strictly, be regarded as a form of litigation.

LOCAL AUTHORITY

England and Wales are divided for the purposes of local government into a number of local authorities. The primary division is into counties (some of which are Metropolitan and some non-Metropolitan) and the secondary division is into districts. There is also a third division into parishes (known in Wales as communities), but no effective power is vested in these tertiary authorities. Some authorities are also entitled to the ancient title of Borough, but this confers status and does not materially affect the powers and responsibilities of the authority.

The constitution and conduct of local authorities is currently governed by the Local Government Act 1972. It was formerly the case that contracts entered into by local authorities had to be under seal, but the Corporate Bodies (Contracts) Act 1960 dispensed with this requirement.

All contracts made by or on behalf of a local authority must be made in accordance with its standing orders but it is not incumbent upon any party contracting with a local authority to ensure that the standing orders have been complied with, nor does non-compliance with such orders invalidate any contract entered into by or on behalf of the local authority. An officer of a local authority may have both actual and ostensible authority to contract on behalf of it.

See Law Report: *Carlton Contractors v Bexley Corporation* (1962).

LOCATIONAL BILL OF QUANTITIES

See Bill of Quantities.

LOSS AND EXPENSE

The phrase 'direct loss and/or expense' is used in the JCT Conditions of Contract to identify those financial losses or expenditures which a contractor under such agreement may seek to recover as a consequence of material disturbance of the regular progress of the works by specified causes.

In the absence of any judicial interpretation, it is suggested that whilst 'expense' might relate to identifiable payments made by the contractor but the benefit of which he has been denied as a direct consequence of some qualifying event (eg the rent paid for portable office buildings during a site shut-down), 'loss' might have a wider application and embrace loss of some part only of the total benefit which the contractor might reasonably have expected to obtain from some expenditure (eg loss of the full productive output of an item of mechanical plant due to intermittent stoppages).

A problem arises with the above distinction, however, when 'direct loss and/or expense' is contrasted with the phrase 'direct loss and/or damage', which is that incorporated in the schedule which governs the respective rights and liabilities of the parties upon determination by the contractor of his employment under the contract.

As determination has a much more fundamental effect than disturbance, it presumably follows that 'damage' is wider than expense — which creates the difficulty of finding a different meaning for the two expressions. Alternatively, the omission of 'expense' from 'direct loss and/or damage' suggests only that its use in 'loss and/or expense' is tautological.

See Damages. Law Report: *A & B Taxis Ltd v Secretary of State for Air* (1922).

LOSS OF PROFIT

Profit is one element of damages which one party to a contract may seek to recover as a direct consequence of some breach of contract by the other party. It is essential, however, to prove that the loss has been sustained, or at least that there is a demonstrable probability that the breach has directly denied the aggrieved party the opportunity to earn some measure of profit.

Where an employer intends to use the completed contract works for a profit-making activity, the deferment of which beyond the contract date for completion will result in measurable loss, then such loss should form an element of any liquidated damages provisions of the contract. If there is no provision for liquidated damages, then the test will be whether or not a loss of such nature was in the contemplation of the contracting parties as being a likely result of a breach of their contract at the time they entered into it.

It is of course the case that any financial damage (being, in the terms of the JCT Conditions of Contract, a 'loss' or 'expense') suffered by a contractor as a direct consequence of some breach by the employer can be viewed as loss of profit, if only by virtue of a commercial definition of profit being an excess of income over related expenditure. However, where a breach of contract by the employer results in the delayed completion of the contract works as a direct consequence of which the contractor is forced into the continued deployment upon the contract works of resources which could demonstrably be employed more profitably elsewhere, then such loss, if proved, can form an element of his claim for damages arising from such breach. It must always be borne in mind, however, that an aggrieved party faced with a breach by the other has a duty to mitigate the consequences of such breach.

LUMP SUM CONTRACT

See Contract.

MAIN CONTRACT

The term 'main' is used to distinguish a primary contract between an employer and a contractor from any related subsidiary agreement between such main contractor and sub-contractor.

MAINTENANCE

It is common in construction contracts to require the contractor to make good at his own expense any defects which appear in the completed works after handing over and for some specified period thereafter and which are rendered necessary by some breach of contract on the part of the contractor.

This specified time is sometimes inaptly termed the 'maintenance period'; but the even less apt phrase 'defects liability period' is used by the JCT Conditions of Contract. Sufficient to say that a contractor's liability for any defects attributable to him can extend beyond the 'period' in question.

The ICE Conditions of Contract use the term 'period of maintenance' but any defects arising from fair wear and tear are specifically excluded from the contractor's liability, thus pointing up the imprecision of the term 'maintenance' — which strictly is the act of preserving something unimpaired regardless of the cause.

See Limitation.

MAINTENANCE PERIOD

See Maintenance.

MATERIALS

In construction contracts this term is used to mean all physical matter incorporated in the works, embracing manufactured articles as well as naturally occurring substances. Sometimes the phrase 'materials and goods' is used but this is a tautology for no such definitive distinction can be drawn, except perhaps in the case of materials arising from excavations and having no economic value and which cannot therefore be classed as goods.

Whilst it is common practice for the employer to specify with some precision the materials to be used by the contractor, in the absence of such precision, or where a contract is silent as to the materials to be used, there is an implied warranty that they shall be of good quality. Such warranty corresponds to the warranty of merchantability under the Sale of Goods Act 1979.

See Law Reports: *Young & Marten Ltd v McManus Childs* (1968); *Croudace v Cawoods* (1978).

MEASURE AND VALUE CONTRACT

See Contract.

MEASUREMENT

A dimension or the act of ascertaining such dimension. Dimensions obtained by measurement are used to calculate quantities of constructional work, materials and components. In this context enumeration is considered to be measurement.

The Standard Methods of Measurement used by the construction industry are in reality classifications of constructional work and only partly concerned with measurement as such.

The term 'admeasurement' was used by the ICE Conditions of Contract until the fifth edition, from which it was dropped in favour of the more commonly used 'measurement'.

MEASUREMENT CONTRACT

See Contract.

MISREPRESENTATION

A false statement of material fact made by one party to another in the course of negotiations leading to a contract and which, whilst not intended to be a binding term, is intended to induce the contract. A fraudulent misrepresentation is made knowingly or without belief in its truth, or recklessly, careless of whether it be true or false. An innocent misrepresentation is made with an honest belief in its truth and may or may not contain elements of negligence. Where an inducement to contract is not the result of a positive act but rather of some failing, then it is not technically a misrepresentation and may be actionable in tort as negligence.

The general consequence of misrepresentation is to render a contract voidable or rescindable. Where the misrepresentation is fraudulent it will give cause for an action in tort for deceit. An innocent misrepresentation may also give cause for the recovery of damages under Section 2 of the Misrepresentation Act 1967.

See Law Reports: *Carlill v Carbolic Smoke Ball Co* (1893); *Esso Petroleum Co Ltd v Mardon* (1976).

MISTAKE

The common law recognises only 'operative' mistake, being a mistake of material fact which prevents the formation of a contract and which will result in an ostensible contract being declared void by the court.

There are several categories of operative mistake: the common mistake is a misconception shared by both parties either as to the existence of the subject matter of the agreement or as to a fact fundamental to it; mutual mistake occurs when the parties negotiate at complete cross-purposes as to the identity of the subject matter of the agreement; unilateral mistake may be over the identity of the person contracted with, over the expression of intention by one party or over the nature of a document signed by one of the parties.

Where there is no operative mistake but a party has contracted under a misconception, such party may in appropriate circumstances obtain equitable relief from his contractual obligations.

See Law Reports: *Roberts & Co Ltd v Leicestershire County Council* (1961); *Radford v De Froberville* (1977).

MOBILIZATION CHARGES

See Overheads.

MONOPOLY

The exclusive possession of the trade in some commodity.

MUTUAL DEALINGS

Both the Companies Acts and the Bankruptcy Act 1914 contain provisions which permit the aggregation of mutual debts and mutual credits which exist between a solvent and an insolvent company or individual in order to establish the net balance of a mutual dealings account which will then be the only sum at issue between the parties. These provisions afford important protection for the solvent party and are pertinent to the Construction Industry in so far as it is common practice for there to be mutual dealings between main contractors and their suppliers and sub-contractors. The mutual dealings provisions would also enable a claim for breach of contract to be set off against claims by a liquidator or trustee.

On the grounds that Section 31 of the Bankruptcy Act 1914 should be interpreted as not applying only to mutual debts, mutual credits and mutual dealings which arise out of contract, but also to liabilities owed to the taxation authorities, a summons brought by the liquidator in the voluntary winding-up of D H Curtis (Builders) Ltd (1977) seeking a declaration that HM Customs and Excise was not entitled to set-off, against their obligation to repay the company a sum of value added tax, claims against the company by the Inland Revenue and the Department of Health and Social Security were dismissed.

NEGLIGENCE

Negligence is a tort and concerns the general duty to take care which exists quite apart from and usually in addition to contractual obligations. It results when one party who owes a duty to another to do something, or to forbear from doing something, is careless in the discharge of that duty, as a consequence of which the other party suffers material damage.

For many years it was necessary in English law for a party to have suffered physical damage to person or property in order to recover the consequential financial loss from the negligent party, but the decision in the case of *Hedley Byrne v Heller* (1964) established that a negligent mis-statement of fact which resulted in indirect financial loss could give rise to liability. The distinction drawn by this case between financial and physical damage has been, it is argued, appreciably modified by the decisions in *Anns v Merton* (1977), *Esso Petroleum v Mardon* (1976), and *Batty v Metropolitan Properties* (1978). The effect of these cases (two of which were concerned with liability for building works) has been appreciably to extend the ambit of tortious liability in English law, and to render largely ineffective any contractual protection which a party may have sought to give himself *vis-à-vis* another contracting party.

The degree of care to be exercised is related to the ostensible skill and knowledge of a person who holds himself out as being competent in some sphere of activity. Where the plaintiff in an action for negligence is himself careless he may find himself unable to recover some part of the financial loss which he has sustained on the ground that there had been contributory negligence by him.

See Law Report: *Arenson v Cassan, Beckman, Rutley & Co* (1975).

NEGOTIATED CONTRACT

See Contract.

NOMINATED

This term is used by all the major standard forms of building and civil engineering contract to identify suppliers and sub-contractors with whom the employer wishes the principal contractor to contract. The act of nomination does not of itself create any contractual obligation between the nominator and the nominated and notwithstanding any preliminary negotiations that may have taken place between an employer (or his architect or engineer) and an intended sub-contractor, or supplier of goods, the contracts entered into between the principal contractor and such nominated sub-contractors or suppliers, will be governed exclusively by the terms of such contracts.

See Nomination.

NOMINATION

In substance the standard forms of construction contract all reserve to the building owner the right to nominate (via his agent) certain specialists for particular work which is part of the overall job. It is then anticipated that, subject to certain rights of objection, the main contractor will employ these specialists as his sub-contractors to carry out the relevant work as part of the project as a whole.

The smooth operation of this nomination system is frequently upset for all sorts of reasons, such as a failure by the main contractor to exercise his rights of objection; a sense of unity with the architect rather than the contractor on the part of the specialist; and above all because of problems about who is to design and be responsible for the specialist's work — the architect (as provided by the main contract and expected by the main contractor) or the specialist (as expected by the architect and as very often happens in fact).

When for one reason or another an initial nomination is rendered abortive, re-nomination becomes necessary. A classic case dealing with re-nomination is *Bickerton v NW Regional Hospital Board* (1969), where the nominee went into liquidation and the main contractor demanded a fresh nomination by the architect. This was refused, presumably because it was believed that a re-nomination would almost certainly lead to an obligation on the part of the building owner to pay the price demanded by the re-nominee. In the absence of the re-nomination the main contractor did the work himself and was subsequently paid the original nominee's price — which was less than the cost the main contractor had incurred. The main contractor then successfully sued for the shortfall as damages for breach of the implied obligation of the architect to re-nominate. The House of Lords held that the implication was essential to make sense of the nomination provisions of the JCT Conditions of Contract, since it was impossible, in light of the wording of the clauses, for the architect to expend the prime cost sum in favour of the main contractor; accordingly there must always be a nominee (or re-nominee) in whose favour the sum could be expended. It is to be noted as being of particular importance that one of the key steps in the reasoning leading to this conclusion was the proposition that the main contractor had no right to do work covered by prime cost sums. This decision creates problems for the building owner which the major standard forms of construction contract have attempted to meet in different ways.

The Joint Contracts Tribunal significantly amended the relevant clauses in the 1980 edition of its Conditions and also published Standard Forms of Collateral Agreement to be entered into by specialists and building owners — a solution which has the merit of recognising in formal terms what was often the factual situation; however, the existence of three contracts — each with only one party in common with the others — highlights the difficulties which result when it becomes necessary to translate a dispute into terms of whom to sue and for what. On the other hand the ICE Conditions of Contract have been amended to incorporate a set of complicated provisions the legal effect of which is to place on the employer's shoulders a large degree of financial responsibility for the conse-quences of nominating specialists, and whose practical effect will probably be to reduce the frequency with which the nomination system is employed. The GC/Works/1 Conditions of Contract deal with the problem in the simplest way by giving the contractor a very broad right of objection, and subject to the exercise of that right (at the proper time) by putting responsibility for all the consequences of nomination expressly upon the contractor.

The sort of problems created by the nomination process are particularly well illustrated by the cases of *Harrison v Leeds* (1980) and *George Taylor & Co v G Percy Trentham* (1980). In Harrison's case, a decision that a nomination of a specialist whose tender stipulated for free access to a level site for the first nine months of the main contract period, operated also as an instruction to postpone the main contracts works (other than the specialist works) was upheld by the Court of Appeal. In Trentham's case a building owner, following a practice note of the Joint Contracts Tribunal and withholding sums from a nominated sub-contractor's certified entitlement under the main contract, on the basis of delay by the nominated sub-contractor (there being a direct warranty between the building owner and the nominated sub-contractor), lost to an application for summary judgement by the main contractor.

NOTICE

A notice is a formal intimation or warning of something. Notices are frequently required in connection with the carrying out and administration of building and civil engineering contracts. It is important strictly to comply with any terms and conditions relating to them for two reasons. Firstly, provision for notice to be given to a particular party is usually made so as to ensure that the recipient is warned of the existence or possibility of some matter or event in respect of which he may wish, or have, to take steps to protect himself. Secondly, the party by whom the notice is to be given may find he has irretrievably destroyed his right to relief by failing to give the appropriate notice.

See Law Report: *Tersons Ltd v Stevenage Development Corporation* (1963).

NOVATION

The assignment of obligations arising out of a contract cannot be made without the consent of the party entitled to performance of the obligations. The contracting parties must agree to the substitution of a third party, the third party must consent to the substitution, and there must be some consideration for it. This effectively substitutes a new contract for the old one and the transfer is known as a contract by novation.

See Law Reports: *Chandler Bros v Boswell* (1936); *Chatsworth Investments Ltd v Cussins (Contractors) Ltd* (1969).

NUISANCE

The tort of nuisance is the wrong done to a person by unlawfully disturbing him in the enjoyment of his property or in the exercise of some common right. Public nuisance is that which affects the community at large and is a criminal offence which only creates a civil cause of action for the individual where that individual suffers specific damage over and above that of the general public. Private nuisance affects only one or a determinate number of persons and gives grounds for civil proceedings only.

Nuisance is quite frequently encountered in connection with building and civil engineering contracts, but the law takes a commonsense view of building operations, accepting that they must go on — providing they are reasonably carried out and that reasonable precautions are taken to minimise their nuisance value. The common causes of such nuisance are noise, odour, dust and dirt, water and sometimes vibration.

Although nuisance committed in the course of a construction contract is evidently caused directly by the execution of the works, an injured party will frequently seek a legal remedy not only from the contractor but also from the employer (and also a sub-contractor if such be involved). For this reason it is usual for an employer to require a contractor to indemnify him against claims (including nuisance) arising from the carrying out of the works. Such an indemnity does not absolve an employer from his tortious liability but provides him with a subsequent remedy against the contractor. In the case of construction contracts the remedy for nuisance is more frequently to be found in an injunction to remove the cause than in damages.

See Law Reports: *Harrison v Southwark & Vauxhall Water Co* (1891); *Andreae v Selfridge & Co Ltd* (1938).

OBSCURITIES

An agreement the terms of which are so obscure as to be incapable of having a practical meaning assigned to them will be unenforceable as a contract. Where an expression has more than one meaning the court will not, in the absence of appropriate evidence, speculate as to the intention of the parties. Although a court may receive evidence in an attempt to resolve an ambiguity in the terms of an agreement, should it conclude that the obscure term is quite meaningless that term will be disregarded and the rest of the agreement, providing it is clear enough, will be enforced.

Where an agreement drawn up by one of the parties to it is in some respect ambiguous, it may be possible to invoke the so-called *contra proferentem* rule in order to have the interpretation of the originator rejected. This will not apply to the use, at the suggestion of one party, of any standard form of contract conditions.

See Law Report: *Tersons Ltd v Stevenage Development Corporation* (1963).

OBSTRUCTION

See Prevention.

OCCUPATION

The act of taking possession, especially of a place or of land. In construction contracts the term is sometimes used to refer to the re-possession by the employer of the land on which the contract works have been carried out and to the employer's usage of the constructed works. During the construction of the works it appears to be the case that the employer grants the contractor a licence to occupy the land, which occupation is frequently referred to as possession. The nature, effect, and in particular the revocability of such a licence is a matter of some difficulty — as appears from the discussion in the case of *Hounslow v Twickenham Garden Developments* (1971). Occupiers have well defined responsibilities under the law, but as between the specific parties to a contract these may be limited or transferred by express agreement.

See Legislation: Defective Premises Act 1972; Occupier's Liability Act 1957.

OFFER

An offer is a spoken or written proposal from one person to another. If accepted (ie agreed to) by the other without qualification, the offer and acceptance constitute the contract created by the acceptance. If the response to the offer is qualified or varies the terms of the offer, it is not an acceptance but a counter-proposal, called by lawyers a counter-offer. Until there is a valid offer and acceptance there is no binding contract. The actual word 'offer' need not be used and terms such as 'estimate', 'quotation' or 'tender' will have the same effect.

An offer must be distinguished from an invitation to treat, which as its name suggests does no more than ask for negotiations to be started. Thus if a building contractor (by tendering) 'accepts' an invitation to tender made by a prospective employer, there is probably no binding contract between the two; the employer has invited tenders and/or negotiations which the contractors may or may not take up.

See Formation. Law Reports: *Routledge v Grant* (1828); *Falck v Williams* (1900); *Peter Lind & Co v Mersey Docks and Harbour Board* (1972).

OFFICIAL REFEREE

Although technically the office no longer exists, old habits die hard and the circuit judges who are now specially charged with the work previously done by official referees may conveniently be so called. The three main official referees are in London, although they can and do sit elsewhere. This is helpful, for it enables the interlocutory steps in an action to be taken in London, where the lawyers often are, whilst permitting the trial to be held closer to the locality which is most convenient to the parties and their witnesses.

Amongst other work, the official referees deal with building and engineering disputes involving any technical or accounting complication. The right of appeal from a decision of an official referee is restricted, much as it is in arbitration proceedings, to questions of law. However, where there is a charge of fraud or of a breach of professional duty, an appeal will lie both on questions of fact and law.

In cases before an official referee it is common to schedule in great detail the precise items in dispute and to set against each item the comments of the parties. This Official Referee's or Scott's Schedule is frequently expensive to produce but it facilitates the trial of the action.

OMITTED WORK

Work can be said to have been omitted from a construction contract under three main circumstances. First; where the employer or his agent order work to be omitted in exercise of powers granted expressly by the contract conditions. Second; where the contractor fails to carry out work which he is under contract to execute. Third; where work essential to a project is not expressly referred to in the contract bills of quantities, specification or other record of the agreement. Each of these circumstances gives rise to different considerations, which are discussed below.

1   A contract will usually give the employer, his architect or engineer express power to order the omission of part of the contract works and provide for the consequent adjustment of the contract price. In the absence of such an express term the implied power to omit work may be very hard to establish. Such a provision only contemplates genuine and complete omissions; in the case of *Gallagher v Hirsh* (1899) it was held that such a term could not be used by an employer to divert work to another contractor. When adjusting the contract price in respect of omitted work regard must be had to the precise terms of the contract. These may prescribe the rate to be applied to each unit quantity of omitted work and they may provide for the revaluation of remaining work, the cost of executing which has been influenced by the omission.

2   The omission by a contractor of anything other than small, unimportant, items would prevent substantial completion which, in the case of an ordinary lump sum contract, he must achieve before he becomes entitled to payment. Where a contract specifies entire completion the whole must be finished in every detail before any payment will be due. These rules may be expressly modified so as to permit the right to instalment payments, are most unlikely to be enforceable where the contractor has been prevented by the employer from completing the work, cannot be enforced where there can be shown to be an implied promise to pay for whatever work has been done, or in the event of frustration or impossibility of performance after the employer has received a valuable benefit from what has been done. In the case of contracts other than for a lump sum a contractor may be entitled to be paid for the work he has done but this may be balanced by a counter-claim for damages by the employer because of non-completion of the whole. The rule of substantial completion will normally apply to a measurement and value contract.

3   In the case of contracts which employ bills of quantities to define the quality and quantity of the contract works (eg the JCT Conditions of

Contract), such omitted work will usually be admitted to be a variation and the contract price will be adjusted accordingly. In the case of contracts based on drawings and specifications, however, even when bills of quantities are provided, the decision whether or not to supplement the contract price will turn on the true construction of the agreement in question.

See Extra Work, Variation. Law Report: *Hoenig v Isaacs* (1952).

OPERATIONAL BILL OF QUANTITIES

See Bill of Quantities.

ORDER

See Instruction.

OVERHEADS

A contraction of 'overhead costs', referring to those èxpenses of an enterprise the amount of which is independent of the quantity of work done by the enterprise — such as office staff salaries, as distinct from the wages and other emoluments of labourers and tradesmen; and office rents and rates, as distinct from the rents for production plant hire.

In construction contracts the term is frequently used loosely to embrace all the foregoing costs and is sometimes qualified by 'head-office' or 'site' to distinguish those output-unrelated costs which are incurred in respect of the organisation generally as distinct from those of a specific project. The term does not, however, have a precise meaning, and whether or not a particular expense is recoverable as part of a specific claim is, in the absence of agreement between the parties, a matter for decision by the court.

Overheads are sometimes also referred to as establishment charges and mobilisation charges although these terms more accurately refer to those expenses which whilst project-related are independent of the quantity of work to be executed.

OWNERSHIP OF GOODS AND MATERIALS

There are two basic rules which it is important to get clear:
1 What is permanently fixed to a building or land or incorporated into the construction of a permanent building becomes the property of the owner of the land or building.

2 Subject to rule 1 , no-one can transfer to someone else a better right to property than he himself has.

This latter rule can best be illustrated by an example. Many construction contracts provide that the building owner can in certain circumstances (eg on the appointment of a receiver) take over and use the plant and equipment which the contractor has assembled to do the work. However, the contractor can only effectively give this right of use to the employer if he has it himself; and if the contractor has hired plant, the full extent of his rights are governed by the terms of the hire contract — which may provide that in the circumstances (ie the appointment of a receiver) the hire ends. If it does, then the contractor is left with no right which he can effectively transfer to the building owner or which the building owner can use. It follows from rule 2 that the question of what rights have been transferred and what have not can be extremely difficult to answer. It also follows that answering this question is primarily a problem of working out what the contract intends to happen by reference to various rules developed by statute and the courts to assist.

As regards goods and materials, the strong fundamental rule is that, subject to a term in the contract to the contrary, they remain the property of the contractor until they are incorporated into the works and thereby become affixed to the land. Once they are incorporated, the property in the materials passes to the freeholder, although as against the contractor or sub-contractor they are the property of the respective employer. Once the property has passed, the contractor has no right to remove or to reclaim the materials, although this will be implied in the situation where the builder has some further business to do in connection with the works (eg repairing or remedying them) and for which purpose he needs to remove or replace goods or materials.

Any provisions in the contract relating to the ownership of materials and goods should be examined carefully as these will override the general law. A common provision, and one to be found in Clause 16 of the JCT Conditions of Contract, is one providing for the payment for materials upon their delivery to site or on certification of their delivery, and in this case the property passes when payment or certification occurs — again of course subject to the rule that the contractor cannot grant the property in the goods to the owner unless he (the contractor) has himself obtained property in the goods.

On completion the builder will normally have a right to remove any goods and materials he did not ultimately need, if they have not been used in or fixed to the works, even if initially ownership did pass to the building owner. This implied right exists as regards unused materials (and also all plant) even where there was an express provision in the contract transferring ownership under the delivery or certification provisions mentioned above.

See Law Reports: *Aluminium Industrie Vaassen B V v Romalpa Aluminium Ltd* (1976); *re Bond Worth Ltd* (1979). Legislation: Sale of Goods Act 1979.

PARTNERSHIP

Partnership involves a contract between the partners to engage in a business with a view to profit. The contract will often be in writing but does not have to be; it may be implied from the circumstances. It is, however, wiser to have a written contract so that the risk of misunderstandings over such questions as the proportions in which profits or losses are to be shared can be minimised.

Partnership carries with it in most cases the danger of unlimited liability on the part of the partners. This is the main difference from the use of a company for trading. The basic code for partnership is statutory — the Partnership Act 1890. What each partner contributes to the partnership depends of course on circumstances, but it will usually be property, skill or labour; none of these is essential, however.

PATENT DEFECT

A term used in contra-distinction to latent defect and meaning a defect which is, or which would be upon inspection, immediately apparent.

PC

See Prime Cost.

PENALTY

The parties to a contract often agree to the inclusion of a clause which provides that a fixed and agreed sum, known as a 'liquidated' sum, shall be paid as damages for any particular breach of contract. If the agreed sum, whatever it might be called in the contract, is construed as a penalty, it will not be enforced by the courts.

The question to be determined is whether the parties intended to make a genuine pre-estimate of the damage likely to ensue from the particular breach. If the answer is yes, then the clause provides for liquidated damages, whatever they have been called, and is enforceable. In that event it does not matter at all what the injured party's actual damage is, nor even if it be the fact that he has in the event suffered none; he is entitled to the agreed liquidated damages — no more, no less. If, on the other hand, the intention is to secure performance of the contract by frightening one party through the imposition of a fine or penalty, then the sum is a penalty whatever it might have been called. Thus any sum must not be extravagant or unconscionable in comparison with the greatest loss, or unrelated to any loss, that might follow upon the breach. If it is, it is a penalty and is unenforceable; and the injured party is entitled to his actual damage, if any, no more, no less.

If the breach is a non-payment of money, any sum stipulated which is greater than that owed is a penalty, as it cannot be a genuine pre-estimate of the loss. There is a tendency to construe as a penalty a provision calling for the payment of a single lump sum. Similarly the same rate for breaches of different potential magnitude is likely to be regarded as a penalty. There may be a penalty if the clause purports to forfeit the retention money on the occasion of a breach of contract. It will often be unfair because the sum of retention money increases with no relation to the completion price, and also it will normally increase as the cost of the remaining work decreases.

See Law Reports: *Dunlop Pneumatic Tyre Co v New Garage Co Ltd* (1915); *Peak Construction (Liverpool) Ltd v McKinney Foundations Ltd* (1970).

PERFORMANCE BOND

See Bond.

PERSONAL INJURY

Personal injury means, naturally enough, injury to one's person as opposed to one's property — the blow rather than the theft. It includes disease and any impairment of a person's physical or mental condition; thus frightening or intimidating a person is 'causing injury'.

It is to be noted that a defendant takes his victim as he finds him. For example, if you negligently drive into someone there is clearly going to be liability since negligence of that sort will cause some injury. However, it may happen that the injured person is particularly prone to injury. The classic example is the man with the 'eggshell' skull; the head injury he suffers is likely to be much greater than that suffered by a person with a skull of normal thickness; but the defendant is liable for the injury as such and is not entitled to limit his liability to the damages which might have been expected from normal circumstances.

PERSONAL REPRESENTATIVE

This is the term given to a person who deals with the affairs of another who is dead. Personal representatives are either executors — appointed by the deceased's will, or administrators — appointed by the court.

PLAINTIFF

This is the word used to describe the person or company who initiates a High Court action. It is the one who wants something — very often money; but sometimes it is other things such as a declaration as to rights; an order restraining someone else from doing something; an order making someone else do something. The party against whom such proceedings are brought is called the defendant. In arbitration the respective parties are called claimant and respondent.

PLANNING CONSENT

The main provisions governing the use of land in England and Wales are contained in the Town and Country Planning Act 1971 (as amended from time to time) and any proposed development needs planning permission. A few sorts of development (eg the expansion of a private house by a limited amount) have automatic permission under a General Development Order (GDO) of 1977 (as amended). The 23 classes of development covered can be found in the First Schedule, Part 1, of the GDO. For cases outside these specified classes the vital question is whether what the developer plans to do is a 'development' within the Act.

Various regulations set out the manner in which a planning application must be made. Thus particulars and plans and drawings must accompany the application and various notices will need to be served preceding the application. The local planning authority decides any applications and an aggrieved party may appeal to the Secretary of State for the Environment. Any point of law may be appealed to the High Court.

Precisely what is and what is not development can be an extremely difficult question to answer, and it is not one which it would be appropriate to deal with here. However, in practical terms, it is probably best to assume that planning permission is necessary until told otherwise, and when in any doubt to take professional advice.

PLANT

In the context of building contracts, plant includes all the items which are to be used for the purpose of the construction of the works but which will not form part of the permanent structure on completion. Plant may be unfixed (eg tools and light machinery) – in which case the contractor remains, *vis-à-vis* the employer, the owner throughout. Alternatively plant may be temporarily affixed to the land or the building (eg scaffolding, formwork, site huts) – in which case, and in the absence of express provisions in the contract, it is uncertain, having regard to the law of ownership, to whom the property belongs during the period of affixation.

As is the case with goods and materials, clauses in the contract may provide for the ownership of, and the passing of property in, plant. These seizure and vesting clauses operate in basically the same way for plant as they do for materials.

If the contractor's plant expressly vests in the employer it is presumably implied that it will re-vest in the contractor on completion. Similarly, if ownership vests in the employer by virtue of the fact of affixation to the land, then presumably a term can be implied in the contract giving the contractor the right to remove the plant when it is no longer needed, and in any event on completion, and re-vesting title in him on removal.

See Hire, Hire Purchase, Ownership of Goods and Materials.

PLEADINGS

This term is used to describe the key formal documents in civil litigation or arbitration. For example the party initiating proceedings sets out in a Statement of Claim (litigation) or a Points of Claim (arbitration) the basic facts upon which he proposes to rely as contributing to the claim.

In order to plead a breach of contract one must:
1 identify the parties
2 define the contract
3 identify the term broken
4 plead that the breach caused damage
5 claim the damage, specifying what it is.

The other party then sets out the facts he relies upon in a Defence (litigation) or Points of Defence (arbitration) and may make a Counter-Claim. This may prompt a Reply (and if appropriate a Defence to the Counter-Claim). In addition each party may ask for Particulars (ie the supply in writing of more detail spelling out some obscure part of the case). The names of the pleadings in arbitration are also used by the Commercial Court.

The pleadings should be a succinct statement of the facts and should not be set out in the form of evidence; very lengthy detail should not be included but should be set out in a schedule and annexed to the relevant pleading. Neither is it necessary (although it is often helpful) to spell out contentious questions of law which the tribunal will be asked to determine. It follows naturally that requests for particulars which go to evidence or law are not permissible.

POSSESSION

See Occupation.

POSSESSORY LIEN

See Lien.

POSTPONEMENT

In the absence of an express term in the contract the employer has no power to postpone any part of the works. To allow him to do so, in the absence of such a provision, would enable him to dictate the way in which the contractor carries out the works — a course which is also denied the employer unless the contract expressly permits him to do so. Given that there is such a provision (eg JCT Conditions of Contract Clause 23.2) then the extent of the employer's power, and the consequence of a postponement, fall to be decided by reference to the provisions of the contract.

See Interference. Law Report: *Harrison v Leeds* (1980).

PRECEDENT

See Courts.

PRELIMINARIES

A common contraction of 'preliminary clauses', meaning descriptive items which appear in specifications and bills of quantities and which do not refer directly to the physical work which is the subject of the contract but rather to general matters concerning the circumstances in which the work is to be carried out and the provision of facilities such as site huts, supervisory staff, water for the works, temporary lighting and power, insurances and the like. Although these items traditionally precede the items of measured work and are in such sense 'preliminary', it will be seen that the items themselves describe obligations which are often not so much preliminary as continuous.

Preliminary items frequently give rise to difficulty when valuing variations. The measurement and valuation of varied work is usually provided for in the contract and in a contract with bills of quantities it is normally priced at the rates or prices contained in the bills. However, whereas the prices for the measured work can, within reason, be considered to be directly proportional to the given quantities — making the application of the rates a simple matter — the prices for the preliminary items will not have this direct relationship with the quantities of measured work and will need to be adjusted to take account of the effect of the varied work upon the 'preliminary' obligations.

In a contract without bills of quantities it is usual to find a provision that any varied work shall be paid for at rates contained in a schedule incorporated in the contract; such rates are to be taken as being inclusive of all 'preliminary' obligations.

94

PREVENTION

A particular and extreme form of interference.

See Law Report: *Cory (William) & Sons v London Corporation* (1951).

PRIME COST

Frequently abbreviated to PC, prime cost is a phrase which is best specifically defined in any particular contract. However, when no such definition appears, the parties will presumably agree that prime cost is related to work to be done by a sub-contractor and not by the main contractor, and would construe the expression as meaning a net charge passed to the sub-contractor by the contractor. If the parties do not agree, and a dispute centres on the meaning of the phrase, then evidence would normally be adducible to show what the generally accepted meaning in the industry is. If such evidence were convincing, the court could rely upon this meaning unless it proved impossible to reconcile such meaning with the expressed terms and/or the circumstances surrounding the making of the agreement.

The JCT Conditions of Contract use the term without defining it but the ICE Conditions of Contract do so, as does the Standard Method of Measurement of Building Work. It is doubtful whether this latter definition can be considered to be incorporated in a contract under the JCT Conditions by virtue of the provisions of Condition 2.2.2 (which require the Contract Bills to have been prepared in accordance with the rules of the Standard Method of Measurement) but it could be advanced in support of the evidence of common usage.

See Daywork.

PRIVITY OF CONTRACT

The doctrine by which the only parties who can enforce rights or liabilities under a contract are the parties to it, a principle which was once critical but which is now of declining importance as Parliament and the courts combine to create a new doctrine of general liability.

If A and B agree that A will pay C a sum of money, the only person who can sue A for non-performance is B; C has no right of action on the agreement. Another example is the architect or engineer who is not normally a party to the construction contract which he administers and owes no-one any obligation under such contract. He may, however, owe the building owner obligations, but this will be under the terms of his contract of employment.

The extensions of general liability have rendered the doctrine of privity substantially less important, and indeed the absence of a contractual link may in some cases help the prosecution of a claim rather than hinder it, such as where the intervening contracts have bars to action, as in the case of *Sharpe v Sweeting* (1963).

PROOF OF EVIDENCE

A formal written statement in which a person sets out facts and matters which he can swear are within his personal and direct knowledge. In the case of an expert witness, the proof of evidence may also contain his opinions on relevant topics.

The document is for the use of the party calling the witness and the other side may only have access to it by agreement.

It is to be noted that the proof of an expert witness will not necessarily be identical with the report which he will also have to tender in advance as a condition imposed on a party wishing to call him. This is because the proof may go further and contain comments on the other side's expert reports, on matters to be considered for the purposes of cross-examination, and on other like matters.

QUALIFIED ACCEPTANCE

See Acceptance.

QUANTITY SURVEYOR

Traditionally one who was concerned with the measurement and valuation of construction work, but currently the practice of quantity surveying extends well beyond these basic activities. Neither use of the title nor exercise of the functions of quantity surveying are restricted by the law, but only members of the Royal Institution of Chartered Surveyors are legally entitled to the designation Chartered Quantity Surveyor, and to the use, in association with their names, of the letters FRICS or ARICS — meaning Fellow and Associate respectively of the Institution. Other organisations which cater for quantity surveyors are the Incorporated Association of Architects and Surveyors and the Institute of Quantity Surveyors; qualified members of these bodies may style themselves 'Incorporated Quantity Surveyors'.

Modern quantity surveying is concerned with the financial and economic aspects of construction. Its activities extend from the provision, for the prospective building owner, of reports on feasibility, through early stage estimates and cost-planning of the evolving design, into the preparation of bills of quantities, the obtaining and evaluation of tenders, the negotiation of contractual arrangements and the complete administration of the financial aspects of construction contracts. Within construction firms quantity surveyors provide the commercial counterparts to the above and sometimes undertake project planning and production management.

The JCT and the GC/Works/1 Conditions of Contract provide for the naming of the quantity surveyor who will execute specific functions under the terms of the contract. Although the quantity surveyor will usually be engaged and remunerated by the employer under such contract, in the discharge of his functions he must act impartially.

See Law Report: *Tyrer v Monmouthshire County Council* (1974).

QUANTUM MERUIT

This phrase means 'what it is worth' and the term is applied in those cases where no specific price has been agreed, or in the very rare cases where the specified price has ceased to be applicable. The convenient English phrase is a 'reasonable sum'.

A 'reasonable sum' is a fair price for doing the work as at the date the work is done. A starting point is of course the actual cost of the work, but clearly the duty to pay a reasonable price does not oblige the building owner to pay for inefficiency.

There are three contractual situations where payment is to be of a reasonable sum: (1) where there is an express agreement to pay a reasonable sum for the work; (2) where there is an agreement to do work and, whilst it is obviously intended that payment should be made, no sum is stipulated by way of payment; (3) where the contract pricing mechanism has been vitiated by the events which have occurred; this is very rare.

A 'reasonable sum' settlement will be imposed under the Law Reform (Frustrated Contracts) Act 1943 where the payment of such sums as the court considers just may be awarded for work done under the contract before it was frustrated and thereby ended. In such a case the payments and the claim for such a sum will normally be ascertained by reference to what is reasonable, having regard to the value to the employer of the work done.

In the rare cases where extra work is ordered and done outside the ambit of the contract, it will give rise to a right on the contractor's part to be paid a reasonable sum. In very special circumstances work which is done in advance of the conclusion of an agreement may fall to be paid for on a reasonable sum basis and may not be subject to valuation in accordance with these subsequently agreed terms.

See Law Reports: *Lacey (Hounslow) v Davis* (1957); *Trollope and Colls and Holland and Hannen and Cubits v Atomic Power Construction* (1963).

QUOTATION

A term sometimes used in contra-distinction to 'estimate' to indicate a firm offer to execute work or supply goods for a price and not merely an indication of a likely price. It should be noted, however, that an estimate may well, in the absence of an express statement to the contrary, be regarded as a valid offer and not merely an approximation or indication of the probable cost of works or goods. Similarly, a quotation within which the sum quoted is expressly declared to be an approximation and not a firm offer cannot result in a fixed price contract simply by virtue of an acceptance.

RATES

This term has two substantial meanings relevant to the industry. The first is the charge per unit which a contractor makes for doing work; for instance, for the work of supplying and fixing tiles to a wall he may want an overall figure for the whole of the work (ie a price) or he may want to be paid a set sum per unit of area (ie a rate). Similarly the contractor may wish to charge the work by reference to the labour employed and the materials used, in which case rates will be attached to the hours of work and the unit quantities of materials.

The other meaning is the charge levied by a local authority for the use or occupation of land. A contractor in possession of a site may well be an occupier, and therefore liable for rates, even if no site huts or similar temporary accommodation is erected. If site huts are erected there is no question but that the contractor is an occupier and responsible for the payment of rates.

RATIO DECIDENDI

See Courts.

REASONABLE

It has been said that this is one of those words which everyone knows the meaning of but which no-one finds easy to define. This paradox derives from the fact that one man's 'reasonable' is another man's 'extreme' — it is a relative term which relies for its definition upon a value judgement. Thus to the man who did the work, the row of tiles wavering slightly at it crosses the floor has been laid to a reasonable standard of workmanship, while to the building owner it is unacceptable.

The effect of using the word in construction contracts is to give to the person who finally determines what is reasonable (be he architect, arbitrator or judge) a measure of discretion — albeit a discretion which must be exercised with regard to the material evidence put before him. Thus a judge will hear witnesses for both sides and decide which view he prefers in all the circumstances of the case.

RECITALS

This term describes the statements of (usually background) fact which often appear at the commencement of a formal document. For example, an arbitrator's award will usually recite, *inter alia*, the fact that disputes arose between the parties and were referred to arbitration, that the arbitrator was duly appointed, and that he had duly carried out the arbitration — usually indicating the manner in which this was done. The award will then go on to the operative part, namely the decisions which the arbitrator has reached.

A construction contract will often recite the background to its making (eg that the employer is desirous of having certain works executed and has caused drawings and bills of quantities showing and describing the work to be done) — before it goes on to the operative part of the agreement which contains the substantive obligations of the parties and identifies those who will have a role to play under the contract, such as the architect and quantity surveyor.

RECTIFICATION

A technical term relating to the situation which arises when a party to a written contract, or a contract recorded in writing, contends that the document does not accurately record what was in fact agreed and consequently requires it to be corrected. If the other party agrees with this contention then it can be put right without reference to the court; it is only when the other party resists the correction that proceedings for rectification are necessary and may be taken.

The conditions which have to be satisfied before the court will grant rectification are stringent and accordingly this relief is rarely granted. For practical purposes it is necessary to show that prior to the signing of the document there was a concluded agreement which embodied (or excluded, as the case may be) the contended term. Further, the party seeking rectification must show exactly what amendment would have to be made to the agreement in order for it to record the precise intention of the parties.

A manifest error or omission on the face of a written agreement may be put right by the court as a matter of construction; this is not rectification.

See Law Reports: *Managhan County Council v Vaughan* (1948); *A Roberts & Co Ltd v Leicestershire County Council* (1961); *American Airlines Inc v Hope* (1974).

REGULAR PROGRESS

The basic obligation to be implied into all construction contracts, where there is no express obligation (which will presumably only be in connection with the smallest of projects), is that the contractor must execute the work within a reasonable time. By itself such an obligation will not impute an agreement on the part of the contractor to engage in regular progress, albeit that irregular progress might well provide evidence that the time eventually taken to complete was unreasonable.

All major construction contracts will have express provisions for the times of commencement and of completion, and the question of whether or not the contractor is bound to engage in regular progress with the works will depend upon the associated provisions of such contracts.

REGULATIONS

This term embraces the large and increasing body of what can loosely be called 'rules' by which the government, local authorities and statutory bodies exercise control over what may and what may not be done in all sorts of fields.

The construction industry is affected by a great number of these rules and it is particularly to be noted that a statutory duty is imposed on contractors to comply with the building regulations by the building regulations themselves — an imposition which in due course will be overtaken and reinforced by Section 72 of the Health and Safety at Work Act 1974.

Clauses 6 and 26 respectively of the JCT and ICE Conditions of Contract refer expressly to the contractor's obligation to conform with regulations and give some indication of the scope of this term.

REINSTATEMENT

This term is in common usage but has two particular meanings within the context of construction contracts. The more general refers to the re-establishing of a physical condition which existed or which ought to have existed, and is used in reference to the opening up and subsequent making good of a public highway or other road — where failure to reinstate may result in damage or injury to persons or property and where, consequently, it is wise expressly to allocate liability as between the employer and the contractor.

The second meaning refers to the re-employment of a contractor following the automatic determination of his employment consequent upon his committing an act of bankruptcy, as provided by Clause 27.2 of the JCT Conditions of Contract.

REMEDY

In the context of the law and of the construction industry this term covers any one or more of the various sorts of relief which can be given by a court or other tribunal to alleviate or cure the consequences of acts or omissions of others.

Damages is the usual remedy for breach of a construction contract. The alternative of specific performance is very rarely given in the context of such contracts due to the natural reluctance of the courts to become involved in what may amount to the task of continuous supervision by a judge.

REPRESENTATIVE

See Agent.

REPUDIATION

The repudiation of a contract occurs when one party makes it clear that he does not intend to perform his obligations under it. This may be said in so many words and the other party will then have to consider his reaction. He may 'accept the repudiation' thus treating the contract as at an end and seek only the remedy of damages. On the other hand (subject to the caveat below) he may 'affirm' the contract, in which case he will still be bound by his obligations under it and may then, or later, sue for any loss caused by the breach of contract. However, whilst the contract thus remains in existence the repudiating party may also continue to rely upon the terms of it.

Affirmation may, however, not be possible, for instance where the repudiatory conduct on the part of the building owner has been to sell the land on which the contract was to be executed; in such circumstances the repudiation will have to be accepted.

The affirmation procedure is to be preferred if there is any doubt at all about whether the party at fault has in fact repudiated the contract. This is because the right to rescission only arises where an act or omission is genuinely repudiatory in character, and not merely where someone believed it was, even if the belief was a reasonable one. What is more, the attempt to rescind the contract when the act complained of is not genuinely repudiatory is itself a repudiation.

Breaches of contract by way of negligent omissions or faulty workmanship would not usually amount to repudiation. On the other hand, if a breach effectively prevented the work from being substantially completed, it might well be different; for example, if the contractor abandons the works or if the employer makes completion impossible or refuses to give the contractor possession of the site, the possibility that the act or omission is repudiatory should be carefully considered, as it should be where the breach is of an important term which is characterised by the contract as a 'condition' — in the strict legal sense of the word.

A special situation occurs where time is of the essence of a construction contract (a rare occurrence) and the contractor does not complete on time. The traditional interpretation of 'time is of the essence' is that the injured party is entitled to treat himself forthwith as discharged from his obligations and to exercise his right of rescission. There are, however, practical difficulties in applying this doctrine to a construction contract. What, for example, does one do about the partly constructed buildings? Can the owner use them? Must he pay for them? If so, on what basis? Consequently, such a term in a construction contract should be approached with caution. Where time is not of the essence, any delay by the contractor will not amount to repudiation unless it shows that the contractor does not intend to complete. In such case the employer must tell the contractor that he is treating the delay as a repudiation before dismissing him.

In each case the action of the employer or of the contractor must be looked at in relation to the contract works as a whole and if these actions show that in fact the party does not intend to be bound by, or to carry out, the contract, this will be a repudiation.

See Abandonment, Frustration: *Restitutio in Integrum.* Law Reports: *Heyman v Darwins Ltd* (1942); *Earth & General Contracts Ltd v Manchester Corporation* (1958); *Barker v Wimpey* (1980); *Woodar v Wimpey* (1980).

RESCISSION

When used in relation to misrepresentation this means the setting aside of the contract and the re-establishment of the parties' pre-contractual positions.

Following the breach of a fundamental term of a contract, the aggrieved party may choose to treat such breach as a repudiation of the contract (ie the bringing of it to an end), entitling him to damages. This election for repudiation is also called rescission.

RESTITUTIO IN INTEGRUM

This Latin phrase is a difficult one to render into a felicitous and brief English equivalent. Putting it therefore at some length, it describes a factor which is essential before recission of a contract is possible. Thus for example a would-be purchaser lawfully rescinding a contract to buy land may recover not only any deposit or part payment but also his costs of investigating title and the like; and by such a recovery he is put back precisely into his original position before he entered upon the transaction.

Where restitution to the original position is for practical purposes impossible (even without taking too precise a view of the facts), the recission will not be available and the complaining party is left to such other remedy as he may have, eg for damages for breach of contract. Thus in a case where a complainant had been induced to take shares in a partnership, and the partnership had then been converted into a limited liability company, *restitutio in integrum* was not possible because the shares available to be handed back were not broadly the same as the shares the subject of the initial transaction.

The concept is rather technical but important in a number of fields of law.

See Repudiation.

RESTRICTIVE COVENANT

See Covenant.

RETENTION

This word, and the associated phrase 'retention fund', is used to describe the sums of money notionally retained by the employer from the contractor (or by a contractor from a sub-contractor) from the amounts payable for work already done. The purpose of the retention is to provide a fund from which the employer will be able, if necessary, to recoup the cost of having defects repaired which might appear in the work and which the contractor is unwilling to put right — a procedure which is designed to give the contractor an incentive to do the repair work by under-paying him for what has been done and making payment of the balance dependent upon the execution of the repairs.

In addition to the foregoing basic scheme, the JCT Conditions of Contract also endeavour to give additional protection to the contractor by imposing a trust on the retention fund, the point being that monies held in trust would not go into the creditor's pool in the event of the insolvency of the employer. In practice it is very rare that a separate retention fund is created by the retaining party, the amount of the retention merely serving to reduce the demand on the retaining party's financial resources. Because of this, there is no real protection given to the contractor, since, for the trust provision to be effective, a separate and identifiable fund must be specifically established.

See Law Report: *Re Tout & Finch* (1954); *Rayack v Lampeter* (1979).

REVOCATION

The withdrawal of an offer before it is accepted. Where a party has, for example, offered to do work, and has subsequently decided to withdraw — perhaps because he has under-priced or under-estimated his other commitments — he may revoke the offer at any time before it is accepted. This is done by informing the party to whom the offer has been made (ie the offeree) that it has been withdrawn (ie revoked). However, if the offeree has sent off his acceptance (even if the offeror has not received it) before the news of the withdrawal reaches him, then the acceptance is effective and the revocation is not. For the revocation to be effective it must reach the offeree before the acceptance has been made — which effectively is when the latter is despatched.

It is to be noted that tenders often state a period for which they are to remain open for acceptance. If a tender is, exceptionally these days, under the seal of the offeree then it cannot be withdrawn until such period expires. However, if the tender is, as is usual, not under seal, it is doubtful whether there is any obligation to keep it open for acceptance for a requisite period, unless it can be shown that a preliminary contract has been made establishing that the right to tender was only granted on condition that the offer would be left open for the requisite period.

See Law Report: *Byrne v Van Tienhoven* (1880).

RIBA FORMS OF CONTRACT

This is an out-moded reference to the Standard Forms of Building Contract issued by the Joint Contracts Tribunal. The title derives from the fact that the forms are published by the Royal Institute of British Architects which is also a member of the Joint Contracts Tribunal.

SCHEDULE OF RATES

A contractual basis for valuing construction work, consisting of a series of descriptive items identifying obligations or work to be done by a contractor and against each of which a money value is entered by him. Such a schedule may be created on an *ad-hoc* basis or, as in the case of the Schedule of Rates for Building Works of the Property Services Agency of the Department of the Environment, be published for general use.

It is very common to see schedules of rates incorporated on contracts which are not based on bills of quantities — so as to provide a basis for valuing any variations which may be ordered.

SCOTT SCHEDULE

Sometimes called an 'Official Referee's Schedule', this is a very detailed listing of all items in dispute between litigants and against which the comments of the respective parties are entered. The object is to reduce the complexity of disputes involving technical or accounting complications and thus facilitate trial of the action. The schedule may be ordered by a judge or by an arbitrator or it may be prepared by agreement between the parties in dispute.

See Official Referee.

SCOTT v AVERY CLAUSE

See Arbitration.

SEALED OFFER

See Costs.

SEIZURE

See Vesting.

SERIAL CONTRACT

See Contract.

SERVICE

Used in the context of notices and the like (eg a notice determining the contractor's employment), this means the formal act of delivery of such notice. The contract terms may require a particular mode of service (eg by hand or by recorded delivery post) and may specify where service has to be made; in such cases the particular requirements must be followed for the notice to be effective.

Notices which are posted by the ordinary mails will be assumed to have arrived in the normal course of the post (ie when the Post Office say it should have arrived) — unless the contrary is proved. Consequently it is most unwise to entrust a document of importance to the ordinary mails; it should be delivered by hand or sent by recorded delivery post.

SET-OFF

Under this term it is convenient to deal with what are in fact two separate concepts with a common effect, namely set-off and diminution. Set-off is the term used to describe the right of one party to a contract to set off against an otherwise justified claim by the other party the cost consequence of a breach of the same or a closely related contract by such other party. Thus a purchaser of goods who receives them late will, in the absence of special circumstances, be obliged to pay the price of the goods but can set off the damages he has incurred by reason of the late delivery. The right of set-off is implied by the general law but it can be excluded by express agreement. The important case of *Bernard Sunley and Sons Ltd v Mottram Consultants Ltd* (1975) established that the crossing out of an express right of set-off in a printed form of contract was sufficient to exclude that right.

Diminution occurs where, for example, a contractor executes poor quality work the value of which, to the employer, is thereby diminished. Whether the reduced sum consequently payable by the employer is seen as the original price less the cost of having the work put right, or whether it is seen as a diminished price for work of reduced value, is of purely academic interest, for the financial effect in each case is the same.

See Mutual Dealings. Law Reports: *Hanak v Green* (1958); *Gilbert-Ash (Northern) Ltd v Modern Engineering (Bristol) Ltd* (1973).

SETTLEMENT

The amicable resolution of disputes without need of litigation or arbitration is in the public interest, and once a dispute has been settled by agreement the courts will be very reluctant to interfere. However, it is to be noted that there must be a specific agreement with a quid pro quo from each side made for the purpose of resolving an extant dispute. Thus if the parties are litigating or arbitrating with each other about matter A and they work out a compromise of A, that compromise will not prevent litigation or arbitration about matter B unless the compromise contains a relevant term, such as one waiving all claims arising out of the transaction as a whole, which clearly covers the issue.

A settlement must be distinguished from a mere preamble to the operation of the contractual machinery. Thus a contractor might claim an extension of time, might thereafter discuss his claim with the architect and might agree to accept a reduced period of extension. Thereafter the architect makes an extension of time of the agreed period. However, such an agreement is not a settlement, for it has not been made with the express intention of resolving a dispute but merely in the normal exercise of administrative functions, and either party to the contract would be perfectly entitled, in normal circumstances, to seek to persuade an arbitrator to review the extension of time granted.

SIMPLE CONTRACT

See Contract.

SITE

In the absence of an express definition in the contract, this term means the place where the permanent construction work is to be located. However, the term should not be left undefined, since it is often of great importance to know the exact extent of the site, not least so that the contractor can evaluate the problems of access and security and so that the owner knows what he is obliged to hand over to the contractor for the purposes of the contract works.

The danger is that, physically on the ground, the 'natural and obvious' extent of the site is considered to be quite clear and as a result everyone assumes that that is what it is under the contract. Such a course is most unwise; the contract should be checked for a definition. If there is one, it should be compared with the 'natural and obvious' site; if there is not, then a suitable definition should be inserted.

SPECIAL CASE

This was a procedure which was available under the Arbitration Act 1950 for dealing with questions of law which one or more of the parties wished to be determined by the courts. An award formulated as a special case consisted of recitals setting out the background to the dispute, findings of fact relevant to the issue, the question of law to be decided, the arbitrator's view of it, and his award on the basis that he was right and his award assuming that he was wrong. It was then for the courts to determine the correct interpretation of the point of law.

See Case Stated.

SPECIALITY CONTRACT

See Contract.

STAGE PAYMENT

See Interim Payment.

STANDARD FORMS OF CONTRACT

There are many standard forms of contract available to the construction industry but by far the best known are those issued by the Joint Contracts Tribunal for building works, by the Institution of Civil Engineers for civil engineering works and by Government for works of either, or both, building and civil engineering; this latter form is known colloquially as 'GC/Works/1'.

Both JCT and ICE forms suffer from the fact that they are an attempt by the parties involved (ie employers and contractors) to reconcile irreconcilable interests. By and large the contractor's interests are better catered for than those of the employer — the best example of this being a comparison of the fourth and fifth editions of the ICE Conditions of Contract.

The Government form, having been prepared unilaterally by an employer, places most of the risks on the contractor and generally speaking is the clearest and best drawn of the common standard forms. Given that identifiable risks are clearly allocated, it will be evident that to place them on the contractor is to ensure that their evaluation is taken into account in tenders and subsequently in the contract sum to be paid by the employer — thus neatly identifying the extent of his total obligations in relation to the works.

A further point to make is that while the standard forms do give rise to problems from time to time, a certain route to even more problems is to amend them piecemeal or to apply them to circumstances for which they are not designed (eg using the JCT 'with quantities' Conditions of Contract for a design and construct or package deal project). The sponsors of the JCT Conditions of Contract have in the past tended to indulge in frequent amendments in response to criticism, with the result that the benefits of continuity were eroded and that further ambiguity was sometimes introduced.

STANDARD METHODS OF MEASUREMENT

Methods of measurement exist for various types of work undertaken by the construction industry. The most common examples are the Standard Method of Measurement of Building Works, the Civil Engineering Standard Method of Measurement, and the Method of Measurement for Road and Bridgeworks issued by the Department of Transport.

The function of these standards is firstly to establish clear rules and principles for the classification, description and measurement of finished work so that bills of quantities based on them can be interpreted with confidence and in the knowledge that, if properly applied, the rules will result in a comprehensive and definitive description of what is required (when tendering) or what has been done (when settling up).

Although originally deriving from the simple measurement of artificers' work, for which purpose standards have existed for over two hundred years, the contemporary objectives of standard measurement are comprehensively to classify construction work – so as separately to identify work of differing complexity and, particularly in the case of the building standard method, the precise description of such work in all its detail. This is necessary to fulfil the role of bills of quantities under the JCT Conditions of Contract in which specifications are not incorporated and where it falls to the bills of quantities to provide the contractual description of the contract work and to define the quality and quantity of such work.

Construction contracts must, of course, expressly provide for the use of a particular method of measurement if such is required. The JCT Conditions of Contract adopt the SMM for Building Works, the ICE Conditions of Contract adopt the Civil Engineering SMM, and the Government contract – GC/Works/1 – leaves the method of measurement to be defined within the bills of quantities themselves.

In the foregoing connection it should be noted that the Conditions of Contract (International) for Works of Civil Engineering Construction (commonly known as the FIDIC Conditions), although incorporating bills of quantities, make no reference to standard measurement except to say in Clause 57 'the works shall be measured net, notwithstanding any general or local custom, except where otherwise specifically described or prescribed in the contract'. Consequently, if bills of quantities are to be supplied by the employer as the basis of competitive tenders, it is highly desirable that the method of measurement underlying such bills be made explicit, and this should be done by the introduction of a suitable clause under the 'conditions of particular application' provisions of Part II of the FIDIC Conditions of Contract.

STATUTE

Statute is another word for 'Act of Parliament'. Statute law is that part of the law which has been formally enacted by Parliament rather than 'declared' or 'made' by judicial decision.

STATUTORY

Being connected with or deriving from a statute. For example, many Acts of Parliament give to Government Ministries the power to make rules (eg the building regulations). These rules are formally promulgated in a document called a 'statutory instrument'.

STAY OF PROCEEDINGS

Proceedings in this phrase means 'proceedings in court' and a stay is a stop to them. The most familiar situation where this occurs, in connection with the construction industry, is when the defendant to an action applies to the court for a stay of proceedings on the ground that the dispute which is the subject of the proposed action is within the ambit of an arbitration agreement existing between the plaintiff and the defendant.

In the case of the JCT or ICE Conditions of Contract — both of which contain an arbitration clause — if an employer sues a contractor for damages for alleged bad workmanship, or a contractor sues an employer for alleged non-payment, the defendant may in either case go to the court and seek a stay of the proceedings so that the dispute may be arbitrated.

It should be noted that the right, in such event, to a stay is circumscribed by certain conditions. For example, the defendant must at all relevant times be ready, willing and able to arbitrate; consequently, a party sued in an action should consider carefully whether he wishes to arbitrate or not before taking a step in the action itself.

SUB-CONTRACT

See Sub-Contractor.

SUB-CONTRACTOR

A person or corporation who enters into an agreement with another (the main contractor) in circumstances in which the object of the agreement (usually called a sub-contract) is ancillary or related to the objects of another agreement (the main contract) to which the main contractor is also a party. Thus there will be a main contract between the building owner and the main contractor and sub-contracts between the main contractor and those whom he wishes to assist him in discharging his obligation by doing work on his behalf or supplying goods and materials to him.

It should be noted that the terms of a sub-contract will usually be construed quite independently of the main contract to which they are related and that a sub-contract which merely says 'the terms of this sub-contract are to be the same as those for the main contract' is probably meaningless. The arrangement whereby a main contractor secures the execution of work by a sub-contractor is sometimes referred to as sub-letting.

See Nomination. Law Reports: *Chandler Bros v Boswell* (1936); *Concrete Construction Ltd v Keidan & Co Ltd* (1955); *Brightside Kilpatrick v Mitchell Construction* (1973); *Winder v Quibell* (1977).

SUBJECT TO COMPLETION

See Acceptance.

SUBJECT TO CONTRACT

This is a phrase which most often occurs in documents which elsewhere appear to record a concluded transaction. The effect is usually to prevent the document being construed as a binding agreement – perhaps because one or other or both of the parties wish to have an opportunity of considering the terms of the contract in their final form before committing themselves. A form of agreement which is so endorsed can finally be concluded by an exchange of letters or by the drafting and execution of a formal contract or by the conduct of the parties in commencing to fulfil their obligations under the contract.

SUBROGATION

See Abrogation.

SUBSTANTIAL COMPLETION

A state of completion of construction works being executed under an entire contract such as will entitle the contractor to payment in respect of such works, even though a deduction might properly be made in respect of any defects.

It is a matter for decision in each case whether or not any defects in performance by the contractor are such as will render the contract not substantially complete.

The doctrine operates to prevent frivolous claims for the non-performance of entire contracts.

See Contract. Law Reports: *Hoenig v Isaacs* (1952); *Bolton v Mahadeva* (1972).

SUPERINTENDING OFFICER

This is the term used in the GC/Works/1 Conditions of Contract to describe the agent of the employer or, in the terminology of these conditions, of the Authority. The Superintending Officer is in substantially the same position as the architect or engineer under the respective JCT or ICE Conditions of Contract — that is to say the extent of his authority and power is determined by the provisions of the particular contract between the Authority and contractor and he is not, of course, a party to the contract. In practical terms, however, the position of the Superintending Officer is stronger than that of the architect or engineer, as many of the provisions of the GC/Works/1 Conditions of Contract make his decision final and binding and not open to review in arbitration.

SUPERVISING OFFICER

As the title 'architect' is protected by law under the provisions of the Architects Registration Act, the JCT Conditions of Contract provide that where the person who is intended to discharge the functions of the architect is not in fact a registered architect, he shall be known as the 'supervising officer'. The difference in nomenclature has no effect on his powers or authority.

See Superintending Officer.

SURETY

See Bond, Guarantee.

TARGET COST CONTRACT

See Contract.

TERM CONTRACT

See Contract.

THIRD PARTY

There are three separate concepts enshrined in this phrase. The first use is to identify the third person in a transaction between three or more. The jargon 'party of the first part, party of the second part, party of the third part ...' is well known. The second use is the one connected with insurance contracts where the third party is by definition not a party to the relevant contract but assumes his status because he has, or alleges that he has, a claim against the insured, or (very rarely) through him, and, by virtue of the insurance contract between the insured and the insurer, a claim against the insurer. The third use is to describe a person brought into litigation by a defendant.

As an example of the third case, a contractor may claim payment for what he asserts was extra work necessary to remedy a defect in the design; this claim is against the employer under the construction contract. The employer may then contend that the remedial work was rendered necessary by initially defective work by the contractor, and may defend the claim on that basis. However, to guard against being proved wrong in his assertion, he may wish to claim in the alternative against his architect for negligent design and therefore joins the architect as a third party in the action with the contractor. The object of this is to ensure that the same tribunal gets to grips with as many as possible of the issues arising out of the same set of facts. In the event of the contractor succeeding in his action against the employer, the tribunal will go on to consider whether the employer's claim of negligence is made out against the architect — who will usually have had the opportunity to attend and take part in the hearing of the action between the contractor and the employer.

A similar situation can arise between employer, contractor and sub-contractor, such as in the case of *Westminster City Corporation v Jarvis* (1970) where the contractor did not bother to attend the House of Lords hearing, knowing that the claim would effectively come to rest with the employer or the sub-contractor — and since both were substantial there was no need to incur the costs of attendance.

TORT

A very difficult word to define with precision but meaning, in broad terms, 'wrong'. More specifically, it is used to describe any one of that group of wrongs which occur by reason of a breach of a civil duty (other than a contractual obligation) which is owed generally among society as a whole or among particular groups. Thus all who drive a vehicle have an obligation to drive carefully. Breach of this obligation may involve both criminal and civil proceedings — the criminal proceedings being brought by the police and the civil proceedings by the injured party. It is in the latter context that lawyers speak of a tort, and of the potential defendant as a tortfeasor or 'wrongdoer'.

The concept has a wide ambit even within the construction industry. It covers negligence, as in the case of *Anns v Merton* (1977) and *Batty v Metropolitan Properties* (1978) and nuisance and trespass, as in the case of *Clay v Crump* (1964).

Where more than one tortfeasor is involved in the same wrong (eg a builder and a local authority in the case of negligently constructed and inspected foundations) and only one party is sued, that party can bring in the other (ie the joint tortfeasor) to make a contribution towards the total recoverable by the plaintiff.

See Legislation: Law Reform (Married Women and Tortfeasors) Act 1935;
Civil Liability (Contribution) Act 1978.

TORTFEASOR

See Tort.

TRADE DISCOUNT

See Cash Discount.

TRADE PRACTICE

See Custom.

TRADE USAGE

See Custom.

TREASURE TROVE

Money, plate or similar articles discovered hidden in the earth or in some other secret place and for so long a time that the true ownership cannot be established. In the event of the owner not being found the Crown is entitled to the treasure but the finder is entitled to the market value of the discovery.

Finds of treasure trove must be reported to a coroner, either directly or through the police. If the objects are not retained by the Crown they will be returned to the finder. It is usual to declare in construction contracts that any such objects found on the site shall, as between the contractor and the employer, be the property of the employer.

TRESPASS

Although the plethora of powers of entry which many statutory organisations enjoy these days make a mockery of it, the basic principle remains that 'an Englishman's home is his castle' and no one is entitled, without leave, to cross the boundaries of another's land. 'Every invasion of private property, be it ever so minute, is a trespass' — *Entick v Carrington* (1765).

The boundaries of land and property exist, in theory, not just at surface level but also at every level of the atmosphere and sub-soil. For this reason special legislation was needed to allow aircraft to fly over land, and a major contractor operating on a tiny urban site with a tower crane, and obliged to let the jib swing free when not in use, was faced with a virtually unanswerable claim of trespass by the adjacent landowners when the jib did swing over their land.

Trespass is not confined to wrongful entry by individuals but can also be committed by placing or allowing materials to get on to neighbouring property. Trespass is a tort and the remedy is damages and/or an injunction to secure discontinuance.

TRUSTEE

One who holds property for the benefit of another. Thus a husband may wish to arrange that on his death his property shall be invested, the resulting income be paid to his wife during her lifetime and the capital to go to his children on her death. He will do this by arranging to have his property transferred to a trustee who will do the investing, pay the income to the wife and ultimately the capital to the children. A person, a group of persons, or a company can act as trustee.

VARIATION

This is a technical usage of the common term and refers to a definable alteration to the nature or extent of contract works or to the conditions under which it has been agreed such contract works will be carried out. The various standard forms of contract provide in differing ways for calculating the financial effect of variations and for consequently adjusting the contract sum.

Standard forms of contract such as the JCT 'with quantities' version contrive to restrict the contract sum to work described and itemised in the contract bills of quantities. Essential work which has, in error, been omitted from the bills of quantites will nevertheless have to be executed by the contractor, but such work will be treated as a variation and its value added to the contract sum.

Where a contract does not incorporate bills of quantities, and where the contract sum has been calculated by reference to drawings and specifications, such sum will, in the absence of an express term to the contrary, be deemed to include everything necessary for the proper completion of the works, whether or not shown or referred to in the drawings and specifications. Thus the subsequent issue of details of essential work will not constitute a variation in the sense in which the term is used in the context of construction contracts.

Terms which permit variations provide a very necessary flexibility to construction contracts and it is inadvisable to omit them since they will not easily be implied by the courts.

See Architect, Extra Work.

VARIATION OF PRICE

This term, sometimes contracted to VOP, is used in some construction contracts to identify conditions which deal with the adjustment of the contract price to take account of fluctuations in the market price of labour and/or materials between the dates of tender and of execution of the works.

See Formula Price Adjustment.

VESTING

Vesting is the result of the transfer of property from A to B. For example, on a transfer of real property A is divested of his estate in the property and B is vested with that estate. This happens when the transfer deed is duly executed and exchanged.

In construction contracts provision is frequently made for the automatic vesting in various parties of the rights in materials or plant upon the happening of certain events. For example, Clause 53(2) of the ICE Conditions of Contract provides that 'all plant, goods and materials owned by the contractor or by any company in which the contractor has a controlling interest shall when on the site be deemed to be the property of the employer'. However, it should be noted that since the most that A can contract to give B is the sum of those rights which A himself has in the property which is the subject of the contract, all that can vest in B is the sum of such rights. Thus if a contract of plant hire provides that on the appointment of a receiver of A the hire will end automatically, then A cannot usually give B any rights in the plant which will remain alive after such an appointment. It is for this reason that the ICE Conditions of Contract incorporate Clause 53(3) which requires all agreements for the hire of plant to contain an undertaking by the hirer to assign the benefit of the agreement to the employer in the event of forfeiture of the main contract.

The exercise of an option to make use of the contractor's plant, goods and materials, such as is provided for by Clause 27.4.1 of the JCT Conditions of Contract, transfers something less than ownership and is sometimes referred to as 'seizure' rather than vesting. It would, however, appear that the essential difference between vesting and seizure is the automatic nature of the former and the optional nature of the latter.

See Ownership of Goods and Materials. Law Report: *Bennet & White (Calgary) v Municipal District of Sugar City* (No 5) (1951).

VEXATIOUSLY

A vexatious litigant is one who goes to court without any real basis to his or her claim and it is to this concept that a court is likely to look to deal with vexatiousness when it is encountered in construction contracts. Accordingly it is reasonable to suggest that it means the baseless employment of a sanction, particularly where the baseless act is repeated. The isolated but baseless use of a sanction, or use when technically the sanction is available but the circumstances make its use wholly inappropriate, are probably covered by the term 'unreasonably', with which 'vexatiously' is often found in tandem.

VICARIOUS LIABILITY

This means liability for the acts or omissions of others. For example a limited company cannot of itself 'do' anything, its entity being metaphysical, and must act through human or mechanical agents — being generally liable for what such agents do or do not do. For example, a company driver D driving a company lorry on company business negligently knocks over and kills a passer-by P. P's executor will be able to sue two defendants — the driver whose liability is personal and the company the liability of which is vicarious. Usually only the company is sued, as private individuals are often thought not to have the necessary money. If, however, the driver was known to have won the football pools, or be a rich eccentric, he might well find himself as joint or even sole defendant.

VICARIOUS PERFORMANCE

This is the converse of vicarious liability. Thus if a company is using human agents to do things for it, it is performing those things vicariously; it therefore has a vicarious liability for the way they are performed. Any one person or body using others as agents is acting vicariously; and although vicarious performance does not always carry vicarious liability it will very often do so.

VITIATE

To vitiate is to invalidate. The most common use of this word in construction contracts is in Clauses 2.2 and 13.2 of the JCT Conditions of Contract. Invalidation of a contract is a most unusual event. Perhaps the clearest examples of it are the sort of Government orders which may be made in wartime in order to prohibit the execution of contracts with nationals of specified countries.

VOIDABLE CONTRACT

See Void Contract.

VOID CONTRACT

The concepts of void and voidable are best considered together; and the easiest example to distinguish the two concepts is the state of marriage. In English law two elements are necessary to a marriage; the first is a valid civil ceremony and the second is consummation. Two people who go through the correct marriage ceremony but who do not consummate it have a voidable marriage. They can either withdraw from the married state at the option of either or they can go on together; they are regarded as married by the law until one or other does withdraw. A marriage which fails to satisfy one of the civil requirements is void from the beginning and this omission cannot be repaired by any degree of con-sumation.

Thus the distinction between a void and a voidable contract is this: a void contract never succeeds in creating rights and obligations while a voidable contract is for all practical purposes a valid and effective contract until one party or the other exercises the right to withdraw.

Examples of void and voidable contracts can be found in the construction industry. For example, a contract to build a brothel may be illegal and therefore void; while in some circumstances a contract entered into in reliance upon a mis-representation (eg by representing an abortion clinic as an hotel) may be voidable by a contractor who has a genuine objection to the practice.

WAIVER

Broadly speaking this term describes the effect (in certain circumstances) of a decision by a party to a contract to forego a right which it possesses under the contract. For example, a building owner may decide that for the sake of effective and speedy administration of a contract he will dispense with the need for the contractor to obtain written confirmation of architect's instructions varying the works. It is, however, very important to note the words 'in certain circumstances' used in the above definition. Contrary to what is believed by many in the construction industry, it is not every such decision which constitutes a waiver.

There are three essential elements to a waiver, all of which must be present:
1 The decision has to be communicated to the other party to the contract.
2 The other party must rely upon it.
3 The other party must prejudice his position by such reliance.

It is also to be noted that a waiver operates as an answer to a particular line of attack. Thus, in the example given above, the contractor may claim to be paid additional money as a consequence of the architect's instructions, only to be met with the defence that he is not so entitled in the absence of written confirmation of such instructions. At that point the contractor may retort, 'You waived the requirement for written confirmation and cannot now pray it in aid'. Waiver never operates as a basis of claim.

See Estoppel. Law Report: *Rickards (Charles) v Oppenheim* (1950).

WAR

War is the most serious of the possible types of human conflict which may affect the execution of contract works. It involves a clash between nations, but no formal declaration of war is necessary. The other types of human conflict can be described by an enormous variety of terms, the most common of which are probably hostilities, insurrection and civil commotion or disorder.

Obviously the foregoing terms overlap to some extent. For instance it is not possible to define the point at which a national strike becomes civil commotion, or at which civil commotion becomes insurrection, or at which hostilities become war. On the other hand hostilities may involve conflict of a limited nature and thus not overlap with insurrection; similarly there may be no relationship between war and civil war.

Most standard forms of construction contract contain provisions dealing with the respective obligations and rights of the parties in the event of war. In the absence of such express provisions, war may well result in frustration of the contract.

WARRANTY

This word has a strict legal meaning and a common usage meaning.

The legal usage describes a secondary term of a contract — the breach of which will not justify repudiation but only give rise to the right to damages. Terms which give an injured party the right to choose between repudiation and damages are properly called 'conditions', but it should be noted that the word 'condition' also has a much more generalised usage.

The common usage employs 'warranty' to describe any term of a contract and quite frequently the contract itself — particularly where the main function of the contract is to guarantee the suitability or quality of work or of a product. In this context it is to be noted that there is a considerable amount of statutory law implying certain warranties into contracts and forbidding any exclusion of them.

A collateral warranty is an independent contract almost always relevant to quality and suitability of goods or work to be supplied and/or done pursuant to a principal contract. The collateral contract is not necessarily between the same parties as the principal contract. For example, a building owner and a nominated sub-contractor may enter into a direct agreement which imposes on them obligations and rights collateral to the rights and obligations existing under the independent contracts which each party will have with the main contractor.

See Guarantee. Legislation: Sale of Goods Act (1979).

WAYLEAVE

Literally translated this word means the 'right to pass'; it describes a right to place on, in or over land some structure — or the temporary right to pass over some land, usually connected with the erection or maintenance of a structure. A common example is the statutory right to wayleaves enjoyed by electricity boards for the construction and maintenance of their chains of pylons across the countryside.

WITNESS

In the course of disputes which reach a court or arbitral tribunal, questions of fact will arise and the court or tribunal will answer such questions by reference to the evidence which it has seen or heard. A large part of that evidence will usually be given orally by the people who have direct knowledge of the facts which are in dispute. These people are called witnesses.

It is important to note that the knowledge of witnesses must be direct, that is to say it must not be second-hand. For example, if a question arose as to what was said in the course of a particular conversation, the only witnesses who would usually be allowed to testify would be the people actually present at the conversation.

See Expert Witness.

WORKING DRAWINGS

This expression encompasses those detail drawings which depict that which is necessary to give effect to the broad design shown on the general drawings. There is no standard practice as to the number and scale of working drawings and much will depend on the complexity of the work involved. However, in the absence of Bills of Quantities, contractors who base their tenders on generalised drawings may be undertaking a substantial responsibility in respect of work which is not shown on the drawings but which is indispensably necessary for completion.

See Contract Documents.

WORKMANSHIP

Workmanship means the degree of skill and care with which work is executed. Many construction contracts will specifically call for a particular standard of workmanship whilst other contracts will require the normal standard implied by the law, namely that work must be undertaken with care and skill, or that the workmanship must be of a reasonable standard. For example, in putting up shelves there is the mechanical question of constructing and fixing the shelves and the ancillary question of whether the appearance and effectiveness of the finished result is appropriate to the job as a whole. Both questions are part of the question — is the workmanship reasonable? It follows that 'workmanship' overlaps with 'design' and with 'suitability of materials' and that contractors should bear this in mind when evaluating what is required of them in any particular case.

A contractor who merely reproduces an architect's or engineer's design without regard for the suitability of such design for its purpose will not, if the design proves defective, escape his obligation to provide a reasonable standard of workmanship. Approaching the matter another way, it is reasonable to assume that the contractor's experience has given rise to a considerable expertise as to the best and most effective way to achieve appropriate results. The benefit of this expertise is part of the service bought by the building owner, and the implicit or implied obligation about workmanship merely means that the building owner is entitled to have that benefit. It is also the case that the more complicated the piece of work, the greater the demands made by the need to achieve a reasonable standard of workmanship.

See Warranty. Law Report: *Young & Marten v McManus Childs* (1968).

BIBLIOGRAPHY

Abrahamson, *Engineering Law & the ICE Conditions* (3rd edn) Applied Science

Burke, J, *Jowitt's Dictionary of English Law* (2nd edn Vols 1 & 2) Sweet & Maxwell

Charlesworth & Cain, *Company Law* (11th edn) Sweet & Maxwell

Duncan Wallace, I.N, *Hudson's Building & Engineering Contracts* (10th edn) Sweet & Maxwell

Guest, A.G, *Chitty on Contracts* (24th edn Gen Ed Vols 1 & 2) Sweet & Maxwell

James, J.S, *Stroud's Judicial Dictionary of Words & Phrases* (4th edn Vols 1 to 5) Sweet & Maxwell

Keating, D, *Building Contracts* (4th edn) Sweet & Maxwell

Parris, J, *The Law & Practice of Arbitration* Geo Godwin

Reynolds & Davenport, *Bowstead on Agency* (14th edn) Sweet & Maxwell

Robb & Brookes, *Outline of the Law of Contract & Tort* Estates Gazette

Walker-Smith & Close, *The Standard Form of Building Contract* Chas Knight

Printed in Great Britain at the College of Estate Management, Reading